EDSTROM

NIGHT

night

ELIE

WIESEL

TRANSLATED FROM THE FRENCH
BY MARION WIESEL

 HILL AND WANG

A DIVISION OF FARRAR, STRAUS AND GIROUX   NEW YORK

Hill and Wang
A division of Farrar, Straus and Giroux
18 West 18th Street, New York 10011

Copyright © 1958 by Les Éditions de Minuit
Translation copyright © 2006 by Marion Wiesel
Nobel Peace Prize Acceptance Speech and Nobel Lecture copyright © 1986
by The Nobel Foundation
All rights reserved
Printed in the United States of America
This English translation originally published in 2006 by Hill and Wang
Commemorative edition, 2017

Grateful acknowledgment is made to the Nobel Foundation for permission to reprint
Elie Wiesel's Nobel Peace Prize Acceptance Speech and Nobel Lecture.

Library of Congress Cataloging-in-Publication Data
Names: Wiesel, Elie, 1928–2016, author. | Wiesel, Marion, translator.
Title: Night : a memoir / Elie Wiesel ; translated from the French by Marion Wiesel.
Other titles: Nuit. English
Description: Commemorative edition. | New York : Hill and Wang, [2017] |
Identifiers: LCCN 2017005124 (print) | LCCN 2017006216 (e-book) |
ISBN 9780374221997 (hardcover : alk. paper) | ISBN 9780374717261 (e-book)
Subjects: LCSH: Wiesel, Elie, 1928–2016—Childhood and youth. | Jews—
Romania—Sighet—Biography. | Holocaust, Jewish (1939–1945)—Romania—
Sighet—Personal narratives. | Sighet (Romania)—Biography.
Classification: LCC DS135.R73 W54813 2017 (print) | LCC DS135.R73 (e-book) |
DDC 940.53/18092 [B]—dc23
LC record available at https://lccn.loc.gov/2017005124

Designed by Abby Kagan

Our books may be purchased in bulk for promotional, educational, or business use.
Please contact your local bookseller or the Macmillan Corporate and Premium Sales
Department at 1-800-221-7945, extension 5442, or by e-mail at
MacmillanSpecialMarkets@macmillan.com.

www.fsgbooks.com
www.twitter.com/fsgbooks • www.facebook.com/fsgbooks

1 3 5 7 9 10 8 6 4 2

CONTENTS

MEMORIAL TRIBUTE

PRESIDENT BARACK OBAMA

JULY 2, 2016

E LIE WIESEL WAS one of the great moral voices of our time, and, in many ways, the conscience of the world. Tonight, Michelle and I join people across the United States, Israel, and around the globe in mourning the loss and celebrating the life of a truly remarkable human being. Like millions of admirers, I first came to know Elie through his account of the horror he endured during the Holocaust simply because he was Jewish. But I was also honored and deeply humbled to call him a dear friend. I'm especially grateful for all the moments we shared and our talks together, which ranged from the meaning of friendship to our shared commitment to the State of Israel.

Elie was not just the world's most prominent Holocaust survivor, he was a living memorial. After we walked together among the barbed wire and guard towers of Buchenwald, where he was held as a teenager and where his father perished, Elie spoke words I've never forgotten—"Memory has become a sacred duty of all people of goodwill." Upholding that sacred duty was the purpose of Elie's life. Along with his beloved wife, Marion, and the foundation that bears his name, he raised his voice, not just against anti-Semitism, but against hatred, bigotry, and intolerance in all its forms. He implored each of us, as nations and as human beings, to do the same, to see ourselves in each other and to make real that pledge of "never again."

At the U.S. Holocaust Memorial Museum that he helped create, you can see his words—"For the dead and the living, we must bear witness." But Elie did more than just bear witness; he acted. As a writer, a speaker, an activist, and a thinker, he was one of those people who changed the world more as a citizen of the world than those who hold office or traditional positions of power. His life, and the power of his example, urges us to be better. In the face of evil, we must summon our capacity for good. In the face of hate, we must love. In the face of cruelty, we must live with empathy and compassion. We must never be bystanders to injustice or indifferent to suffering. Just imagine the peace and justice that would be possible in our world if we all lived a little more like Elie Wiesel.

At the end of our visit to Buchenwald, Elie said that, after all that he and the other survivors had endured, "we had the right to give up on humanity." But he said, "We rejected that possibility . . . We said, no, we must continue believing in a future." Tonight, we give thanks that Elie never gave up on humanity and on the progress that is possible when we treat one another with dignity and respect.

FOREWORD

THE INEXORABLE JOYFULNESS OF ELIE WIESEL

AMBASSADOR SAMANTHA POWER,
U.S. PERMANENT REPRESENTATIVE
TO THE UNITED NATIONS
(2013–2017)

ADAPTED FROM REMARKS DELIVERED
ON NOVEMBER 30, 2016, AT THE
U.S. HOLOCAUST MEMORIAL MUSEUM,
WASHINGTON, D.C.

WORDS TEND TO FAIL US most in two circumstances—in the face of profound evil and of transcendent decency. When Elie Wiesel first tried to describe his experience in the camps, he later wrote, "I watched helplessly as language became an obstacle." We who have the honor to speak about Elie have the opposite challenge, finding words that capture the fierce and magical essence of this marvelous man.

Elie gave friendship with the intensity of a young man fresh out of college—with innocence and adamant conviction that that friendship would be an eternal bond, which, in Elie's case, it usually was. He used to quote someone who said in French, "*Ma patrie, c'est les amis.*" "My friends are my homeland." It was Elie's belief in friendship that relates so powerfully to the miracle of his joyfulness.

Of course, we must consider the context from which that joy somehow emerged. None of us will ever comprehend the depravity of what Elie experienced during the Holocaust. He tried to help us see and feel that pain, but he knew our limits. Nor can most of us fathom the aloneness that Elie experienced after he was liberated from Buchenwald on April 11, 1945. Imagine the sixteen-year-old boy who walked out of those gates. A boy with A-7713 tattooed on his arm.

A boy who, as far as he knew, had lost his entire family, and who—when he gazed at himself in the mirror for the first time since being sent to the concentration camp—saw a corpse staring back at him. "The slightest wind would blow me over," he later said.

Many of us have been struck by the fact that it took Elie ten years to prepare himself to put into words the horrors of what had been done to him and to his family and to his people. A whole ten years before he could begin to write. And when he did so, in the spring of 1955, this wise old man who had been to hell and back was just twenty-six years old. What must it have been like for this man, in his Paris lodgings, to rouse the demons—to hear once again what he called the "silent cries"? "While I had many things to say," he would later write, "I did not have the words to say them . . . How was one to rehabilitate and transform words betrayed and perverted by the enemy? Hunger—thirst—fear—transport—selection—fire—chimney . . . I would pause at every sentence, and start over and over again. I would conjure up other verbs, other images, other silent cries. It still was not right."

He reimmersed himself in that period, into the darkness of night. The approach that came most naturally to him was blunt and unsparing. What he bore witness to—and thus relived—were the horrors inflicted upon him, but also his own most searing moments of dehumanization, when he could not bring himself to help the person whose companionship had helped keep him alive in Auschwitz and later, on the death march—his father. As he eventually wrote, "He had called out to me and I had not answered." In the original text, which Elie wrote in Yiddish, he had added, "I shall never forgive myself."

Elie Wiesel carried all of this. Gathered here, in a museum dedicated to educating people about a systematic effort to eradicate the Jewish people—a museum built upon the testimonies of thousands of survivors, and in whose foundation are etched Elie's words, "For the dead and the living, we must bear witness"—sitting here, it can be hard to imagine that there was a time when the prevailing wisdom was not to bear witness. But that is precisely what it was like when Elie was writing. Survivors did not speak about their past— even to their own children. Here in the United States, there were no memorials to the six million Jews who had been killed. The word "Holocaust" did not even appear in *The New York Times* until 1959. Even in Europe—where the mass murder had taken place and entire Jewish communities had been wiped out—the topic was hardly mentioned. It was against this wall of silence that Elie wrote.

And then the man whose life's mission would be to combat indifference laid his heart out to the world, presented his experiences, his story, and they reacted with indifference. Although he had cut the original Yiddish version from more than eight hundred pages to a little more than one hundred, all the major publishing houses turned the book down. The renowned French novelist François Mauriac resolved to help Elie. "No one is interested in the death camps anymore," publishers told Mauriac. "It just won't sell." When Elie went in search of an American publisher, he later recalled, their rejection letters often noted that American readers "seemed to prefer optimistic books."

All who have read *Night* are haunted, perhaps above all, by Moishe the Beadle. Moishe was among the first wave of foreign Jews deported from Elie's town of Sighet, who were transported by train to a forest in Poland, where they were forced to dig their own graves at gunpoint, and then executed en masse by the Gestapo.

Moishe survived, wounded, faking his death, and eventually made his way back to Sighet, where he told his neighbors what he had witnessed. "Jews, listen to me!" he yells outside the synagogue, weeping. "That's all I ask of you. No money. No pity. Just listen to me!" But no one listens. Moishe is ignored—dismissed as a madman. How cruel was it, then, that young Elie Wiesel, who was taunted by his perpetrators that nobody would ever know or care what had happened to him and his people, how cruel was it that he encountered a world that again seemed indifferent to what he had gone through? When he was trying to place his manuscript, did he feel somehow like Moishe the Beadle, a man who possessed the truth, but was ignored?

And yet none of this appears to have diminished the determination of Elie Wiesel. *Night* of course did eventually find its publishers, and after several years, its readership did begin to grow, at first gradually, and then exponentially. Arguably no single work did so much to lift the silence that had enveloped survivors, and bring what happened in the "Kingdom of Night" out into the light, for all to see. And yet. Injustice was still rampant. Genocide denial against the Armenians, the horrors of his lifetime—Pol Pot, Bosnia, Rwanda, Darfur, Syria in his later years. He lived to see more and more people bear witness to unspeakable atrocities, but he also saw that indifference remained too widespread.

Amid all the pain and disappointment of Elie's remarkable life, how is it that the darkness did not envelop him, or shield him from the sun? How is it that the light in Elie Wiesel's gaze was every bit as defining as his life's experiences? "What is abnormal," Elie once told Oprah Winfrey, "is that I am normal. That I survived the Holocaust and went on to love beautiful girls, to talk, to write, to have toast and tea and live my life—that is what is abnormal."

Elie raged against indifference to injustice, to be sure, but he also savored the gifts of life with ferocious zeal. "We know that every moment is a moment of grace," he once said, "every hour is an offering; not to share them would mean to betray them."

Maybe it was because Elie had such a strong sense of purpose on his journey—to help those who could still be helped. A duty to his neighbor. To the stranger, the stranger that he once was. He called it his eleventh commandment: "Thou shalt not stand idly by . . . You must speak up. You must defend. You must tell the victims, . . . 'You are not alone, somebody cares.' "

Through the years, Elie ventured out to the most unlikely, isolated places. There was Elie in a tiny village along the Thai border with Cambodia, meeting with refugees who had just escaped the Khmer Rouge. There was Elie, crossing the jungle in Nicaragua on foot and in a kayak, to reach the Miskito Indians who had been driven from their land. "I," Elie reflected later, "who have been known to lose my way in my own neighborhood and don't know how to swim," traveled all that way to bear witness to their displacement and see how he could help. Now one might think that in these encounters Elie found only suffering, but he did not. He found meaning. Abe Foxman remembered visiting a school program in Tel Aviv that Elie and Marion had helped set up for undocumented children from Sudan—one of many such initiatives they created— and Abe remembers seeing Elie singing and dancing with the kids, in pure, almost childlike joy.

Elie Wiesel often wrote of the anger within him. But what he projected most effortlessly was his love. Jews, Elie would often say, are a people of unparalleled gratitude—so much so, he pointed out, that they begin the day by thanking God for opening their eyes. Elie's greatest joy came in the time he spent with those closest to him, his wife, Marion, and his son, Elisha.

A few years ago, when he was recovering from heart surgery, Elie was visited by his beloved grandson, Elijah, then just five years old. Here is how Elie describes the encounter: "I hug my grandson and tell him, 'Every time I see you, my life becomes a gift.' Elijah observes me closely as I speak and . . . responds: 'Grandpa, you know that I love you, and I see you are in pain. Tell me: If I loved you more, would you be in less pain?'" Elie writes, "I am convinced God at that moment is smiling as He contemplates His creation."

I am so very sad that my children will not have the chance to talk metaphysics with the master. But before I close, let me offer another reason that God is smiling today. As our nation goes through difficult days, *Night* is a book that is firmly ingrained in that small canon of literature that kids and young adults read when they are growing up in America. If Atticus Finch and Scout are the fictional narrators who help shape our children's moral universe, sixteen-year-old Elie introduces our young to the hard facts of good, evil, and all that lies between.

So, while the void is enormous—above all, for Marion, Elisha, and the rest of the family—and the void is enormous for our world, I too am filled with profound joy knowing that my seven-year-old boy and my four-year-old girl—like Elie's grandkids, and their children after them—will wade into big questions for the first time with Elie Wiesel as their guide. That they will be less alone for having Elie with them. That *Night* will be one of the works that lay the scaffolding for their moral architecture. All because Elie Wiesel was optimistic enough to keep going—and to find the strength to shine his light on us all.

night

THEY CALLED HIM MOISHE THE BEADLE, as if his entire life he had never had a surname. He was the jack-of-all-trades in a Hasidic house of prayer, a *shtibl*. The Jews of Sighet—the little town in Transylvania where I spent my childhood—were fond of him. He was poor and lived in utter penury. As a rule, our townspeople, while they did help the needy, did not particularly like them. Moishe the Beadle was the exception. He stayed out of people's way. His presence bothered no one. He had mastered the art of rendering himself insignificant, invisible.

Physically, he was as awkward as a clown. His waiflike shyness made people smile. As for me, I liked his wide, dreamy eyes, gazing off into the distance. He spoke little. He sang, or rather he chanted, and the few snatches I caught here and there spoke of divine suffering, of the Shekhina in Exile, where, according to Kabbalah, it awaits its redemption linked to that of man.

I met him in 1941. I was almost thirteen and deeply observant. By day I studied Talmud and by night I would run to the synagogue to weep over the destruction of the Temple.

One day I asked my father to find me a master who could guide me in my studies of Kabbalah. "You are too young for that. Maimonides tells us that one must be thirty before venturing into the world of mysticism, a world fraught with peril. First you must study the basic subjects, those you are able to comprehend."

My father was a cultured man, rather unsentimental. He rarely displayed his feelings, not even within his family, and was more involved with the welfare of others than with that of his own kin. The Jewish community of Sighet held him in highest esteem; his advice on public and even private matters was frequently sought. There were four of us children. Hilda, the eldest, then Bea; I was the third and the only son; Tzipora was the youngest.

My parents ran a store. Hilda and Bea helped with the work. As for me, my place was in the house of study, or so they said.

"There are no Kabbalists in Sighet," my father would often tell me.

He wanted to drive the idea of studying Kabbalah from my mind. In vain. I succeeded on my own in finding a master for myself in the person of Moishe the Beadle.

He had watched me one day as I prayed at dusk.

"Why do you cry when you pray?" he asked, as though he knew me well.

"I don't know," I answered, troubled.

I had never asked myself that question. I cried because . . . because something inside me felt the need to cry. That was all I knew.

"Why do you pray?" he asked after a moment.

Why did I pray? Strange question. Why did I live? Why did I breathe?

"I don't know," I told him, even more troubled and ill at ease. "I don't know."

From that day on, I saw him often. He explained to me, with

great emphasis, that every question possessed a power that was lost in the answer . . .

Man comes closer to God through the questions he asks Him, he liked to say. Therein lies true dialogue. Man asks and God replies. But we don't understand His replies. We cannot understand them. Because they dwell in the depth of our souls and remain there until we die. The real answers, Eliezer, you will find only within yourself.

"And why do you pray, Moishe?" I asked him.

"I pray to the God within me for the strength to ask Him the real questions."

We spoke that way almost every evening, remaining in the synagogue long after all the faithful had gone, sitting in the semi-darkness, where only a few half-burnt candles provided a flickering light.

One evening, I told him how unhappy I was not to be able to find in Sighet a master to teach me the Zohar, the Kabbalistic works, the secrets of Jewish mysticism. He smiled indulgently. After a long silence, he said: "There are a thousand and one gates allowing entry into the orchard of mystical truth. Every human being has his own gate. He must not err and wish to enter the orchard through a gate other than his own. That would present a danger not only for the one entering but also for those who are already inside."

And Moishe the Beadle, the poorest of the poor of Sighet, spoke to me for hours on end about the Kabbalah's revelations and its mysteries. Thus began my initiation. Together we would read, over and over again, the same page of the Zohar. Not to learn it by heart but to discover within the very essence of divinity.

And in the course of those evenings I became convinced that Moishe the Beadle would help me enter eternity, into that time when question and answer would become ONE.

———

AND THEN, ONE DAY, all foreign Jews were expelled from Sighet. And Moishe the Beadle was a foreigner.

Crammed into cattle cars by the Hungarian police, they cried silently. Standing on the station platform, we too were crying. The train disappeared over the horizon; all that was left was thick, dirty smoke.

Behind me, someone said, sighing, "What do you expect? That's war . . ."

The deportees were quickly forgotten. A few days after they left, it was rumored that they were in Galicia, working, and even that they were content with their fate.

Days went by. Then weeks and months. Life was normal again. A calm, reassuring wind blew through our homes. The shopkeepers were doing good business, the students lived among their books, and the children played in the street.

One day, as I was about to enter the synagogue, I saw Moishe the Beadle sitting on a bench near the entrance.

He told me what had happened to him and his companions. The train with the deportees had crossed the Hungarian border and, once in Polish territory, had been taken over by the Gestapo. The train had stopped. The Jews were ordered to get off and onto waiting trucks. The trucks headed toward a forest. There everybody was ordered to get out. They were ordered to dig huge trenches. When they had finished their work, the men from the Gestapo began theirs. Without passion or haste, they shot their prisoners, who were forced to approach the trench one by one and offer their necks. Infants were tossed into the air and used as targets for the machine guns. This took place in the Galician forest, near Kolomay. How had he, Moishe the Beadle, been able to escape? By a miracle. He was wounded in the leg and taken for dead . . .

Day after day, night after night, he went from one Jewish house to the next, telling his story and that of Malka, the young girl who lay dying for three days, and that of Tobie, the tailor who begged to die before his sons were killed.

Moishe was not the same. The joy in his eyes was gone. He no longer sang. He no longer mentioned either God or Kabbalah. He spoke only of what he had seen. But people not only refused to believe his tales, they refused to listen. Some even insinuated that he only wanted their pity, that he was imagining things. Others flatly said that he had gone mad.

As for Moishe, he wept and pleaded:

"Jews, listen to me! That's all I ask of you. No money. No pity. Just listen to me!" he kept shouting in synagogue, between the prayer at dusk and the evening prayer.

Even I did not believe him. I often sat with him, after services, and listened to his tales, trying to understand his grief. But all I felt was pity.

"They think I'm mad," he whispered, and tears, like drops of wax, flowed from his eyes.

Once, I asked him the question: "Why do you want people to believe you so much? In your place I would not care whether they believed me or not . . ."

He closed his eyes, as if to escape time.

"You don't understand," he said in despair. "You cannot understand. I was saved miraculously. I succeeded in coming back. Where did I get my strength? I wanted to return to Sighet to describe to you my death so that you might ready yourselves while there is still time. Life? I no longer care to live. I am alone. But I wanted to come back to warn you. Only no one is listening to me . . ."

This was toward the end of 1942.

Thereafter, life seemed normal once again. London radio, which we listened to every evening, announced encouraging news: the daily bombings of Germany and Stalingrad, the preparation of the Second Front. And so we, the Jews of Sighet, waited for better days that surely were soon to come.

I continued to devote myself to my studies, Talmud during the day and Kabbalah at night. My father took care of his business and the community. My grandfather came to spend Rosh Hashanah with us so as to attend the services of the celebrated Rebbe of Borsche. My mother was beginning to think it was high time to find an appropriate match for Hilda.

Thus passed the year 1943.

SPRING 1944. Splendid news from the Russian Front. There could no longer be any doubt: Germany would be defeated. It was only a matter of time—months or weeks, perhaps.

The trees were in bloom. It was a year like so many others, with its spring, its engagements, its weddings, and its births.

The people were saying: "The Red Army is advancing with giant strides . . . Hitler will not be able to harm us, even if he wants to . . ."

Yes, we even doubted his resolve to exterminate us.

Annihilate an entire people? Wipe out a population dispersed throughout so many nations? So many millions of people! By what means? In the middle of the twentieth century!

And thus my elders concerned themselves with all manner of things—strategy, diplomacy, politics, and Zionism—but not with their own fate.

Even Moishe the Beadle had fallen silent. He was weary of talking. He would drift through synagogue or through the streets, hunched over, eyes cast down, avoiding people's gaze.

In those days it was still possible to buy emigration certificates to Palestine. I had asked my father to sell everything, to liquidate everything, and to leave.

"I am too old, my son," he answered. "Too old to start a new life. Too old to start from scratch in some distant land . . ."

Budapest radio announced that the Fascist party had seized power. The regent Miklós Horthy was forced to ask a leader of the pro-Nazi Nyilas party to form a new government.

Yet we still were not worried. Of course, we had heard of the Fascists, but it was all in the abstract. It meant nothing more than a change of ministry.

The next day brought really disquieting news: German troops had penetrated Hungarian territory with the government's approval.

Finally, people began to worry in earnest. One of my friends, Moishe Chaim Berkowitz, returned from the capital for Passover and told us, "The Jews of Budapest live in an atmosphere of fear and terror. Anti-Semitic acts take place every day, in the streets, on the trains. The Fascists attack Jewish stores, synagogues. The situation is becoming very serious . . ."

The news spread through Sighet like wildfire. Soon that was all people talked about. But not for long. Optimism soon revived: The Germans will not come this far. They will stay in Budapest. For strategic reasons, for political reasons . . .

In less than three days, German Army vehicles made their appearance on our streets.

ANGUISH. German soldiers—with their steel helmets and their death's-head emblem. Still, our first impressions of the Germans were rather reassuring. The officers were billeted in private homes, even in Jewish homes. Their attitude toward their hosts was distant but polite. They never demanded the impossible, made no offensive remarks, and sometimes even smiled at the lady of the house. A German officer lodged in the Kahns' house, across the street from us. We were told he was a charming man, calm, likable, and polite.

Three days after he moved in, he brought Mrs. Kahn a box of chocolates. The optimists were jubilant: "Well? What did we tell you? You wouldn't believe us. There they are, *your* Germans. What do you say now? Where is their famous cruelty?"

The Germans were already in our town, the Fascists were already in power, the verdict was already out—and the Jews of Sighet were still smiling.

THE EIGHT DAYS of Passover.

The weather was sublime. My mother was busy in the kitchen. The synagogues were no longer open. People gathered in private homes: no need to provoke the Germans.

Almost every rabbi's home became a house of prayer.

We drank, we ate, we sang. The Bible commands us to rejoice during the eight days of celebration. But our hearts were not in it. We wished the holiday would end so as not to have to pretend.

On the seventh day of Passover, the curtain finally rose: the Germans arrested the leaders of the Jewish community.

From that moment on, everything happened very quickly. The race toward death had begun.

First edict: Jews were prohibited from leaving their residences for three days, under penalty of death.

Moishe the Beadle came running to our house.

"I warned you," he shouted. And left without waiting for a response.

The same day, the Hungarian police burst into every Jewish home in town: a Jew was henceforth forbidden to own gold, jewelry, or any valuables. Everything had to be handed over to the authorities, under penalty of death. My father went down to the cellar and buried our savings.

As for my mother, she went on tending to the many chores in the house. Sometimes she would stop and gaze at us in silence.

Three days later, a new decree: every Jew had to wear the yellow star.

Some prominent members of the community came to consult with my father, who had connections at the upper levels of the Hungarian police; they wanted to know what he thought of the situation. My father's view was that it was not all bleak, or perhaps he just did not want to discourage the others, to throw salt on their wounds:

"The yellow star? So what? It's not lethal . . ."

(Poor Father! Of what, then, did you die?)

But new edicts were already being issued. We no longer had the right to frequent restaurants or cafés, to travel by rail, to attend synagogue, to be on the streets after six o'clock in the evening.

Then came the ghettos.

TWO GHETTOS were created in Sighet. A large one in the center of town occupied four streets, and another, smaller one extended over several alleyways on the outskirts of town. The street we lived on, Serpent Street, was in the first ghetto. We therefore could remain in our house. But, as it occupied a corner, the windows facing the street outside the ghetto had to be sealed. We gave some of our rooms to relatives who had been driven out of their homes.

Little by little life returned to "normal." The barbed wire that encircled us like a wall did not fill us with real fear. In fact, we felt this was not a bad thing; we were entirely among ourselves. A small Jewish republic . . . A Jewish Council was appointed, as well as a Jewish police force, a welfare agency, a labor committee, a health agency—a whole governmental apparatus.

People thought this was a good thing. We would no longer have to look at all those hostile faces, those hate-filled stares. No more fear. No more anguish. We would live among Jews, among brothers . . .

Of course, there still were unpleasant moments. Every day, the Germans came looking for men to load coal into the military trains. Volunteers for this kind of work were few. But apart from that, the atmosphere was oddly peaceful and reassuring.

Most people thought that we would remain in the ghetto until the end of the war, until the arrival of the Red Army. Afterward everything would be as before. The ghetto was ruled by neither German nor Jew; it was ruled by delusion.

SOME TWO WEEKS before Shavuot. A sunny spring day, people strolled seemingly carefree through the crowded streets. They exchanged cheerful greetings. Children played games, rolling hazelnuts on the sidewalks. Some schoolmates and I were in Ezra Malik's garden studying a Talmudic treatise.

Night fell. Some twenty people had gathered in our courtyard. My father was sharing some anecdotes and holding forth on his opinion of the situation. He was a good storyteller.

Suddenly, the gate opened, and Stern, a former shopkeeper who now was a policeman, entered and took my father aside. Despite the growing darkness, I could see my father turn pale.

"What's wrong?" we asked.

"I don't know. I have been summoned to a special meeting of the Council. Something must have happened."

The story he had interrupted would remain unfinished.

"I'm going right now," he said. "I'll return as soon as possible. I'll tell you everything. Wait for me."

We were ready to wait as long as necessary. The courtyard turned into something like an antechamber to an operating room. We stood, waiting for the door to open. Neighbors, hearing the rumors, had joined us. We stared at our watches. Time had slowed down. What was the meaning of such a long session?

"I have a bad feeling," said my mother. "This afternoon I saw new faces in the ghetto. Two German officers, I believe they were Gestapo. Since we've been here, we have not seen a single officer . . ."

It was close to midnight. Nobody felt like going to sleep, though some people briefly went to check on their homes. Others left but asked to be called as soon as my father returned.

At last, the door opened and he appeared. His face was drained of color. He was quickly surrounded.

"Tell us. Tell us what's happening! Say something . . ."

At that moment, we were so anxious to hear something encouraging, a few words telling us that there was nothing to worry about, that the meeting had been routine, just a review of welfare and health problems . . . But one glance at my father's face left no doubt.

"The news is terrible," he said at last. And then one word: "Transports."

The ghetto was to be liquidated entirely. Departures were to take place street by street, starting the next day.

We wanted to know everything, every detail. We were stunned, yet we wanted to fully absorb the bitter news.

"Where will they take us?"

That was a secret. A secret for all, except one: the president of the Jewish Council. But he would not tell, or *could* not tell. The Gestapo had threatened to shoot him if he talked.

"There are rumors," my father said, his voice breaking, "that we are being taken somewhere in Hungary to work in the brick factories. It seems that here we are too close to the front . . ."

After a moment's silence, he added:

"Each of us will be allowed to bring his personal belongings. A backpack, some food, a few items of clothing. Nothing else."

Again, heavy silence.

"Go and wake the neighbors," said my father. "They must get ready . . ."

The shadows around me roused themselves as if from a deep sleep and left silently in every direction.

FOR A MOMENT, we remained alone. Suddenly Batia Reich, a relative who lived with us, entered the room: "Someone is knocking at the sealed window, the one that faces outside!"

It was only after the war that I found out who had knocked that night. It was an inspector of the Hungarian police, a friend of my father's. Before we entered the ghetto, he had told us, "Don't worry. I'll warn you if there is danger." Had he been able to speak to us that night, we might still have been able to flee . . . But by the time we succeeded in opening the window, it was too late. There was nobody outside.

THE GHETTO WAS AWAKE. One after the other, the lights were going on behind the windows.

I went into the house of one of my father's friends. I woke the head of the household, an old man with a gray beard and the gaze of a dreamer. His back was hunched over from untold nights spent studying.

"Get up, sir, get up! You must ready yourself for the journey. Tomorrow you will be expelled, you and your family, you and all the other Jews. Where to? Please don't ask me, sir, don't ask questions. God alone could answer you. For heaven's sake, get up . . ."

He had no idea what I was talking about. He probably thought I had lost my mind.

"What are you saying? Get ready for the journey? What journey? Why? What is happening? Have you gone mad?"

Half asleep, he was staring at me, his eyes filled with terror, as though he expected me to burst out laughing and tell him to go back to bed. To sleep. To dream. That nothing had happened. It was all in jest . . .

My throat was dry and the words were choking me, paralyzing my lips. There was nothing else to say.

At last he understood. He got out of bed and began to dress, automatically. Then he went over to the bed where his wife lay sleeping and with infinite tenderness touched her forehead. She opened her eyes and it seemed to me that a smile crossed her lips. Then he went to wake his two children. They woke with a start, torn from their dreams. I fled.

Time went by quickly. It was already four o'clock in the morning. My father was running right and left, exhausted, consoling friends, checking with the Jewish Council just in case the order had been rescinded. To the last moment, people clung to hope.

The women were boiling eggs, roasting meat, preparing cakes, sewing backpacks. The children were wandering about aimlessly, not knowing what to do with themselves to stay out of the way of the grown-ups.

Our backyard looked like a marketplace. Valuable objects, precious rugs, silver candlesticks, Bibles and other ritual objects were strewn over the dusty grounds—pitiful relics that seemed never to have had a home. All this under a magnificent blue sky.

By eight o'clock in the morning, weariness had settled into our veins, our limbs, our brains, like molten lead. I was in the midst of prayer when suddenly there was shouting in the streets. I quickly unwound my phylacteries and ran to the window. Hungarian police had entered the ghetto and were yelling in the street nearby.

"All Jews, outside! Hurry!"

They were followed by Jewish police, who, their voices breaking, told us:

"The time has come . . . You must leave all this . . ."

The Hungarian police used their rifle butts, their clubs to indiscriminately strike old men and women, children and cripples.

One by one, the houses emptied and the streets filled with people carrying bundles. By ten o'clock, everyone was outside. The police were taking roll calls, once, twice, twenty times. The heat was oppressive. Sweat streamed from people's faces and bodies.

Children were crying for water.

Water! There was water close by, inside the houses, the backyards, but it was forbidden to break rank.

"Water, Mother, I am thirsty!"

Some of the Jewish police surreptitiously went to fill a few jugs. My sisters and I were still allowed to move about, as we were destined for the last convoy, and so we helped as best we could.

AT LAST, at one o'clock in the afternoon, came the signal to leave.

There was joy, yes, joy. People must have thought there could be no greater torment in God's hell than that of being stranded here, on the sidewalk, among the bundles, in the middle of the street under a blazing sun. Anything seemed preferable to that. They began to walk without another glance at the abandoned streets, the dead, empty houses, the gardens, the tombstones . . . On everyone's back, there was a sack. In everyone's eyes, tears and distress. Slowly, heavily, the procession advanced toward the gate of the ghetto.

And there I was, on the sidewalk, watching them file past, unable to move. Here came the Chief Rabbi, hunched over, his face strange looking, without a beard, a bundle on his back. His very presence in the procession was enough to make the scene seem surreal. It was like a page torn from a book, a historical novel perhaps, dealing with the captivity in Babylon or the Spanish Inquisition.

They passed me by, one after the other, my teachers, my friends, the others, some of whom I had once feared, others whom I had found ridiculous, all those whose lives I had shared for years. There they went, defeated, their bundles, their lives in tow, having left behind their homes, their childhood.

They passed me by, like beaten dogs, with never a glance in my direction. They must have envied me.

The procession disappeared around the corner. A few steps more and they were beyond the ghetto walls.

The street resembled fairgrounds deserted in haste. There was a little of everything: suitcases, briefcases, bags, knives, dishes, banknotes, papers, faded portraits. All the things one planned to take along and finally left behind. They had ceased to matter.

Open rooms everywhere. Gaping doors and windows looked out into the void. It all belonged to everyone since it no longer belonged to anyone. It was there for the taking. An open tomb.

A summer sun.

WE HAD SPENT the day without food. But we were not really hungry. We were exhausted.

My father had accompanied the deportees as far as the ghetto's gate. They first had been herded through the main synagogue, where they were thoroughly searched to make sure they were not carrying away gold, silver, or any other valuables. There had been incidents of hysteria and harsh blows.

"When will it be our turn?" I asked my father.

"The day after tomorrow. Unless . . . things work out. A miracle, perhaps . . ."

Where were the people being taken? Did anyone know yet? No, the secret was well kept.

Night had fallen. That evening, we went to bed early. My father said:

"Sleep peacefully, children. Nothing will happen until the day after tomorrow, Tuesday."

Monday went by like a small summer cloud, like a dream in the first hours of dawn.

Intent on preparing our backpacks, on baking breads and cakes, we no longer thought about anything. The verdict had been delivered.

That evening, our mother made us go to bed early. To conserve our strength, she said.

It was to be the last night spent in our house.

I was up at dawn. I wanted to have time to pray before leaving.

My father had risen before all of us, to seek information in town. He returned around eight o'clock. Good news: we were not leaving town today; we were only moving to the small ghetto. That is where we were to wait for the last transport. We would be the last to leave.

At nine o'clock, the previous Sunday's scenes were repeated. Policemen wielding clubs were shouting:

"All Jews outside!"

We were ready. I went out first. I did not want to look at my parents' faces. I did not want to break into tears. We remained sitting in the middle of the street, like the others two days earlier. The same hellish sun. The same thirst. Only there was no one left to bring us water.

I looked at my house, in which I had spent years seeking my God, fasting to hasten the coming of the Messiah, imagining what my life would be like later. Yet I felt little sadness. My mind was empty.

"Get up! Roll call!"

We stood. We were counted. We sat down. We got up again. Over and over. We waited impatiently to be taken away. What were they waiting for? Finally, the order came:

"Forward! March!"

My father was crying. It was the first time I saw him cry. I had never thought it possible. As for my mother, she was walking, her face a mask, without a word, deep in thought. I looked at my little sister, Tzipora, her blond hair neatly combed, her red coat over her arm: a little girl of seven. On her back a bag too heavy for her. She was clenching her teeth; she already knew it was useless to complain. Here and there, the police were lashing out with their clubs: "Faster!" I had no strength left. The journey had just begun and I already felt so weak . . .

"Faster! Faster! Move, you lazy good-for-nothings!" the Hungarian police were screaming.

That was when I began to hate them, and my hatred remains our only link today. They were our first oppressors. They were the first faces of hell and death.

They ordered us to run. We began to run. Who would have thought that we were so strong? From behind their windows, from behind their shutters, our fellow citizens watched as we passed.

We finally arrived at our destination. Throwing down our bundles, we dropped to the ground:

"Oh God, Master of the Universe, in Your infinite compassion, have mercy on us . . ."

THE SMALL GHETTO. Only three days ago, people were living here. People who owned the things we were using now. They had been expelled. And we had already forgotten all about them.

The chaos was even greater here than in the large ghetto. Its inhabitants evidently had been caught by surprise. I visited the rooms that had been occupied by my Uncle Mendel's family. On the table, a half-finished bowl of soup. A platter of dough waiting to be baked. Everywhere on the floor there were books. Had my uncle meant to take them along?

We settled in. (What a word!) I went looking for wood, my sisters lit a fire. Despite her fatigue, my mother began to prepare a meal.

We cannot give up, we cannot give up, she kept repeating.

People's morale was not so bad: we were beginning to get used to the situation. There were those who even voiced optimism. The Germans were running out of time to expel us, they argued . . . Tragically, for those who had already been deported, it would be too late. As for us, chances were that we would be allowed to go on with our miserable little lives until the end of the war.

The ghetto was not guarded. One could enter and leave as one pleased. Maria, our former maid, came to see us. Sobbing, she begged us to come with her to her village, where she had prepared a safe shelter.

My father wouldn't hear of it. He told me and my big sisters, "If you wish, go there. I shall stay here with your mother and the little one . . ."

Naturally, we refused to be separated.

NIGHT. No one was praying for the night to pass quickly. The stars were but sparks of the immense conflagration that was consuming us. Were this conflagration to be extinguished one day, nothing would be left in the sky but extinct stars and unseeing eyes.

There was nothing else to do but to go to bed, in the beds of those who had moved on. We needed to rest, to gather our strength.

At daybreak, the gloom had lifted. The mood was confident. There were those who said:

"Who knows, they may be sending us away for our own good. The front is getting closer, we shall soon hear the guns. And then surely the civilian population will be evacuated . . ."

"They worry lest we join the partisans . . ."

"As far as I'm concerned, this whole business of deportation is nothing but a big farce. Don't laugh. They just want to steal our valuables and jewelry. They know that it has all been buried and that they will have to dig to find it; so much easier to do when the owners are on vacation . . ."

On vacation!

This kind of talk that nobody believed helped pass the time. The few days we spent here went by pleasantly enough, in relative calm. People rather got along. There no longer was any distinction between rich and poor, notables and the others; we were all people condemned to the same fate—still unknown.

SATURDAY, the day of rest, was the day chosen for our expulsion.

The night before, we had sat down to the traditional Friday night meal. We had said the customary blessings over the bread and the wine and swallowed the food in silence. We sensed that we were gathered around the familial table for the last time. I spent that night going over memories and ideas and was unable to fall asleep.

At dawn, we were in the street, ready to leave. This time, there were no Hungarian police. It had been agreed that the Jewish Council would handle everything by itself.

Our convoy headed toward the main synagogue. The town seemed deserted. But behind the shutters, our friends of yesterday were probably waiting for the moment when they could loot our homes.

The synagogue resembled a large railroad station: baggage and tears. The altar was shattered, the wall coverings shredded, the walls themselves bare. There were so many of us, we could hardly breathe. The twenty-four hours we spent there were horrendous. The men were downstairs, the women upstairs. It was Saturday— the Sabbath—and it was as though we were there to attend services. Forbidden to go outside, people relieved themselves in a corner.

The next morning, we walked toward the station, where a convoy of cattle cars was waiting. The Hungarian police made us climb into the cars, eighty persons in each one. They handed us some bread, a few pails of water. They checked the bars on the windows to make sure they would not come loose. The cars were sealed. One person was placed in charge of every car: if someone managed to escape, that person would be shot.

Two Gestapo officers strolled down the length of the platform. They were all smiles; all things considered, it had gone very smoothly.

A prolonged whistle pierced the air. The wheels began to grind. We were on our way.

L YING DOWN WAS NOT AN OPTION, nor could we all sit down. We decided to take turns sitting. There was little air. The lucky ones found themselves near a window; they could watch the blooming countryside flit by.

After two days of travel, thirst became intolerable, as did the heat.

Freed of normal constraints, some of the young let go of their inhibitions and, under cover of darkness, caressed one another, without any thought of others, alone in the world. The others pretended not to notice.

There was still some food left. But we never ate enough to satisfy our hunger. Our principle was to economize, to save for tomorrow. Tomorrow could be worse yet.

The train stopped in Kaschau, a small town on the Czechoslovakian border. We realized then that we were not staying in Hungary. Our eyes opened. Too late.

The door of the car slid aside. A German officer stepped in accompanied by a Hungarian lieutenant, acting as his interpreter.

"From this moment on, you are under the authority of the

German Army. Anyone who still owns gold, silver, or watches must hand them over now. Anyone who will be found to have kept any of these will be shot on the spot. Secondly, anyone who is ill should report to the hospital car. That's all."

The Hungarian lieutenant went around with a basket and retrieved the last possessions from those who chose not to go on tasting the bitterness of fear.

"There are eighty of you in the car," the German officer added. "If anyone goes missing, you will all be shot, like dogs."

The two disappeared. The doors clanked shut. We had fallen into the trap, up to our necks. The doors were nailed, the way back irrevocably cut off. The world had become a hermetically sealed cattle car.

THERE WAS A WOMAN among us, a certain Mrs. Schächter. She was in her fifties and her ten-year-old son was with her, crouched in a corner. Her husband and two older sons had been deported with the first transport, by mistake. The separation had totally shattered her.

I knew her well. A quiet, tense woman with piercing eyes, she had been a frequent guest in our house. Her husband was a pious man who spent most of his days and nights in the house of study. It was she who supported the family.

Mrs. Schächter had lost her mind. On the first day of the journey, she had already begun to moan. She kept asking why she had been separated from her family. Later, her sobs and screams became hysterical.

On the third night, as we were sleeping, some of us sitting, huddled against each other, some of us standing, a piercing cry broke the silence:

"Fire! I see a fire! I see a fire!"

There was a moment of panic. Who had screamed? It was Mrs. Schächter. Standing in the middle of the car, in the faint light filtering through the windows, she looked like a withered tree in a field of wheat. She was howling, pointing through the window:

"Look! Look at this fire! This terrible fire! Have mercy on me!"

Some pressed against the bars to see. There was nothing. Only the darkness of night.

It took us a long time to recover from this harsh awakening. We were still trembling, and with every screech of the wheels, we felt the abyss opening beneath us. Unable to still our anguish, we tried to reassure each other:

"She is mad, poor woman . . ."

Someone had placed a damp rag on her forehead. But she nevertheless continued to scream:

"Fire! I see a fire!"

Her little boy was crying, clinging to her skirt, trying to hold her hand:

"It's nothing, Mother! There's nothing there . . . Please sit down . . ." He pained me even more than did his mother's cries.

Some of the women tried to calm her:

"You'll see, you'll find your husband and sons again . . . In a few days . . ."

She continued to scream and sob fitfully.

"Jews, listen to me," she cried. "I see a fire! I see flames, huge flames!"

It was as though she were possessed by some evil spirit.

We tried to reason with her, more to calm ourselves, to catch our breath, than to soothe her:

"She is hallucinating because she is thirsty, poor woman . . . That's why she speaks of flames devouring her . . ."

But it was all in vain. Our terror could no longer be contained. Our nerves had reached a breaking point. Our very skin was aching.

It was as though madness had infected all of us. We gave up. A few young men forced her to sit down, then bound and gagged her.

Silence fell again. The small boy sat next to his mother, crying. I started to breathe normally again as I listened to the rhythmic pounding of the wheels on the tracks as the train raced through the night. We could begin to doze again, to rest, to dream . . .

And so an hour or two passed. Another scream jolted us. The woman had broken free of her bonds and was shouting louder than before:

"Look at the fire! Look at the flames! Flames everywhere . . ."

Once again, the young men bound and gagged her. When they actually struck her, people shouted their approval:

"Keep her quiet! Make that madwoman shut up. She's not the only one here . . ."

She received several blows to the head, blows that could have been lethal. Her son was clinging desperately to her, not uttering a word. He was no longer crying.

The night seemed endless. By daybreak, Mrs. Schächter had settled down. Crouching in her corner, her blank gaze fixed on some faraway place, she no longer saw us.

She remained like that all day, mute, absent, alone in the midst of us. Toward evening she began to shout again:

"The fire, over there!"

She was pointing somewhere in the distance, always the same place. No one felt like beating her anymore. The heat, the thirst, the stench, the lack of air, were suffocating us. Yet all that was nothing compared to her screams, which tore us apart. A few more days and all of us would have started to scream.

But we were pulling into a station. Someone near a window read to us:

"Auschwitz."

Nobody had ever heard that name.

THE TRAIN did not move again. The afternoon went by slowly. Then the doors of the wagon slid open. Two men were given permission to fetch water.

When they came back, they told us that they had learned, in exchange for a gold watch, that this was the final destination. We were to leave the train here. There was a labor camp on the site. The conditions were good. Families would not be separated. Only the young would work in the factories. The old and the sick would find work in the fields.

Confidence soared. Suddenly we felt free of the previous nights' terror. We gave thanks to God.

Mrs. Schächter remained huddled in her corner, mute, untouched by the optimism around her. Her little one was stroking her hand.

Dusk began to fill the wagon. We ate what was left of our food. At ten o'clock in the evening, we were all trying to find a position for a quick nap and soon we were dozing. Suddenly:

"Look at the fire! Look at the flames! Over there!"

With a start, we awoke and rushed to the window yet again. We had believed her, if only for an instant. But there was nothing outside but darkness. We returned to our places, shame in our souls but fear gnawing at us nevertheless. As she went on howling, she was struck again. Only with great difficulty did we succeed in quieting her down.

The man in charge of our wagon called out to a German officer strolling down the platform, asking him to have the sick woman moved to a hospital car.

"Patience," the German replied, "patience. She'll be taken there soon."

Around eleven o'clock, the train began to move again. We pressed against the windows. The convoy was rolling slowly. A quarter of an hour later, it began to slow down even more. Through the windows, we saw barbed wire; we understood that this was the camp.

We had forgotten Mrs. Schächter's existence. Suddenly there was a terrible scream:

"Jews, look! Look at the fire! Look at the flames!"

And as the train stopped, this time we saw flames rising from a tall chimney into a black sky.

Mrs. Schächter had fallen silent on her own. Mute again, indifferent, absent, she had returned to her corner.

We stared at the flames in the darkness. A wretched stench floated in the air. Abruptly, our doors opened. Strange-looking creatures, dressed in striped jackets and black pants, jumped into the wagon. Holding flashlights and sticks, they began to strike at us left and right, shouting:

"Everybody out! Leave everything inside. Hurry up!"

We jumped out. I glanced at Mrs. Schächter. Her little boy was still holding her hand.

In front of us, those flames. In the air, the smell of burning flesh. It must have been around midnight. We had arrived. In Birkenau.

THE BELOVED OBJECTS that we had carried with us from place to place were now left behind in the wagon and, with them, finally, our illusions.

Every few yards, there stood an SS man, his machine gun trained on us. Hand in hand we followed the throng.

An SS came toward us wielding a club. He commanded:

"Men to the left! Women to the right!"

Eight words spoken quietly, indifferently, without emotion. Eight simple, short words. Yet that was the moment when I left my mother. There was no time to think, and I already felt my father's hand press against mine: we were alone. In a fraction of a second I could see my mother, my sisters, move to the right. Tzipora was holding Mother's hand. I saw them walking farther and farther away; Mother was stroking my sister's blond hair, as if to protect her. And I walked on with my father, with the men. I didn't know that this was the moment in time and the place where I was leaving my mother and Tzipora forever. I kept walking, my father holding my hand.

Behind me, an old man fell to the ground. Nearby, an SS man replaced his revolver in its holster.

My hand tightened its grip on my father. All I could think of was not to lose him. Not to remain alone.

The SS officers gave the order.

"Form ranks of five!"

There was a tumult. It was imperative to stay together.

"Hey, kid, how old are you?"

The man interrogating me was an inmate. I could not see his face, but his voice was weary and warm.

"Fifteen."

"No. You're eighteen."

"But I'm not," I said. "I'm fifteen."

"Fool. Listen to what *I* say."

Then he asked my father, who answered:

"I'm fifty."

"No." The man now sounded angry. "Not fifty. You're forty. Do you hear? Eighteen and forty."

He disappeared into the darkness. Another inmate appeared, unleashing a stream of invectives:

"Sons of bitches, why have you come here? Tell me, why?"

Someone dared to reply:

"What do you think? That we came here of our own free will? That we asked to come here?"

The other seemed ready to kill him:

"Shut up, you moron, or I'll tear you to pieces! You should have hanged yourselves rather than come here. Didn't you know what was in store for you here in Auschwitz? You didn't know? In 1944?"

True. We didn't know. Nobody had told us. He couldn't believe his ears. His tone became even harsher:

"Over there. Do you see the chimney over there? Do you see it? And the flames, do you see them?" (Yes, we saw the flames.) "Over there, that's where they will take you. Over there will be your grave. You still don't understand? You sons of bitches. Don't you understand anything? You will be burned! Burned to a cinder! Turned into ashes!"

His anger changed into fury. We stood stunned, petrified. Could this be just a nightmare? An unimaginable nightmare?

I heard whispers around me:

"We must do something. We can't let them kill us like that, like cattle in the slaughterhouse. We must revolt."

There were, among us, a few tough young men. They actually had knives and were urging us to attack the armed guards. One of them was muttering:

"Let the world learn about the existence of Auschwitz. Let everybody find out about it while they still have a chance to escape . . ."

But the older men begged their sons not to be foolish:

"We mustn't give up hope, even now, as the sword hangs over our heads. So taught our sages . . ."

The wind of revolt died down. We continued to walk until we came to a crossroads. Standing in the middle of it was, though I didn't know it then, Dr. Mengele, the notorious Dr. Mengele. He looked like the typical SS officer: a cruel, though not unintelligent, face, complete with monocle. He was holding a conductor's baton and was surrounded by officers. The baton was moving constantly, sometimes to the right, sometimes to the left.

In no time, I stood before him.

"Your age?" he asked, perhaps trying to sound paternal.

"I'm eighteen." My voice was trembling.

"In good health?"

"Yes."

"Your profession?"

Tell him that I was a student?

"Farmer," I heard myself saying.

This conversation lasted no more than a few seconds. It seemed like an eternity.

The baton pointed to the left. I took half a step forward. I first wanted to see where they would send my father. Were he to have gone to the right, I would have run after him.

The baton, once more, moved to the left. A weight lifted from my heart.

We did not know, as yet, which was the better side, right or left, which road led to prison and which to the crematoria. Still, I was happy, I was near my father. Our procession continued slowly to move forward.

Another inmate came over to us:

"Satisfied?"

"Yes," someone answered.

"Poor devils, you are heading for the crematorium."

He seemed to be telling the truth. Not far from us, flames, huge flames, were rising from a ditch. Something was being burned there. A truck drew close and unloaded its hold: small children. Babies! Yes, I did see this, with my own eyes . . . children thrown into the flames. (Is it any wonder that ever since then, sleep eludes me?)

So that was where we were going. A little farther on, there was another, larger pit for adults.

I pinched myself: Was I still alive? Was I awake? How was it possible that men, women, and children were being burned and that the world kept silent? No. All this could not be real. A nightmare perhaps . . . Soon I would wake up with a start, my heart pounding, and find that I was back in the room of my childhood, with my books . . .

My father's voice tore me from my daydreams:

"What a shame, a shame that you did not go with your mother . . . I saw many children your age go with their mothers . . ."

His voice was terribly sad. I understood that he did not wish to see what they would do to me. He did not wish to see his only son go up in flames.

My forehead was covered with cold sweat. Still, I told him that I could not believe that human beings were being burned in our times; the world would never tolerate such crimes . . .

"The world? The world is not interested in us. Today, everything is possible, even the crematoria . . ." His voice broke.

"Father," I said. "If that is true, then I don't want to wait. I'll run into the electrified barbed wire. That would be easier than a slow death in the flames."

He didn't answer. He was weeping. His body was shaking. Everybody around us was weeping. Someone began to recite Kaddish, the prayer for the dead. I don't know whether, during the history of the Jewish people, men have ever before recited Kaddish for themselves.

"*Yisgadal, veyiskadash, shmey raba* . . . May His name be celebrated and sanctified . . ." whispered my father.

For the first time, I felt anger rising within me. Why should I sanctify His name? The Almighty, the eternal and terrible Master of the Universe, chose to be silent. What was there to thank Him for?

We continued our march. We were coming closer and closer to the pit, from which an infernal heat was rising. Twenty more steps. If I was going to kill myself, this was the time. Our column had only some fifteen steps to go. I bit my lips so that my father would not hear my teeth chattering. Ten more steps. Eight. Seven. We were walking slowly, as one follows a hearse, our own funeral procession. Only four more steps. Three. There it was now, very close to us, the pit and its flames. I gathered all that remained of my strength in order to break rank and throw myself onto the barbed wire. Deep down, I was saying goodbye to my father, to the whole universe, and, against my will, I found myself whispering the words: *"Yisgadal, veyiskadash, shmey raba . . .* May His name be exalted and sanctified . . ." My heart was about to burst. There. I was face-to-face with the Angel of Death . . .

No. Two steps from the pit, we were ordered to turn left and herded into barracks.

I squeezed my father's hand. He said:

"Do you remember Mrs. Schächter, in the train?"

NEVER SHALL I FORGET that night, the first night in camp, that turned my life into one long night seven times sealed.

Never shall I forget that smoke.

Never shall I forget the small faces of the children whose bodies I saw transformed into smoke under a silent sky.

Never shall I forget those flames that consumed my faith forever.

Never shall I forget the nocturnal silence that deprived me for all eternity of the desire to live.

Never shall I forget those moments that murdered my God and my soul and turned my dreams to ashes.

Never shall I forget those things, even were I condemned to live as long as God Himself.

Never.

THE BARRACK we had been assigned to was very long. On the roof, a few bluish skylights. I thought: This is what the antechamber of hell must look like. So many crazed men, so much shouting, so much brutality.

Dozens of inmates were there to receive us, sticks in hand, striking anywhere, anyone, without reason. The orders came:

"Strip! Hurry up! *Raus!* Hold on only to your belt and your shoes . . ."

Our clothes were to be thrown on the floor at the back of the barrack. There was a pile there already. New suits, old ones, torn overcoats, rags. For us it meant true equality: nakedness. We trembled in the cold.

A few SS officers wandered through the room, looking for strong men. If vigor was that appreciated, perhaps one should try to appear sturdy? My father thought the opposite. Better not to draw attention. (We later found out that he had been right. Those who were selected that day were incorporated into the Sonderkommando, the Kommando working in the crematoria. Béla Katz, the son of an important merchant of my town, had arrived in Birkenau with the first transport, one week ahead of us. When he found out that we were there, he succeeded in slipping us a note. He told us that, having been chosen because of his strength, he had been forced to place his own father's body into the furnace.)

The blows continued to rain on us:

"To the barber!"

Belt and shoes in hand, I let myself be dragged along to the barbers. Their clippers tore out our hair, shaved every hair on our bodies. My head was buzzing, the same thought surfacing over and over: not to be separated from my father.

Freed from the barbers' clutches, we began to wander about the crowd, meeting friends, acquaintances. Every encounter filled us with joy—yes, joy: Thank God! You are still alive!

Some were crying. They used whatever strength they had left to cry. Why had they let themselves be brought here? Why didn't they die in their beds? Their words were interspersed with sobs.

Suddenly someone threw his arms around me in a hug: Yehiel, the Sigheter Rebbe's brother. He was weeping bitterly. I thought he was crying with joy at still being alive.

"Don't cry, Yehiel," I said. "Don't waste your tears . . ."

"Not cry? We're on the threshold of death. Soon, we shall be inside . . . Do you understand? Inside. How could I not cry?"

I watched darkness fade through the bluish skylights in the roof. I no longer was afraid. I was overcome by fatigue.

The absent no longer entered our thoughts. One spoke of them—who knows what happened to them?—but their fate was not on our minds. We were incapable of thinking. Our senses were numbed, everything was fading into a fog. We no longer clung to anything. The instincts of self-preservation, of self-defense, of pride, had all deserted us. In one terrifying moment of lucidity, I thought of us as damned souls wandering through the void, souls condemned to wander through space until the end of time, seeking redemption, seeking oblivion, without any hope of finding either.

AROUND FIVE O'CLOCK in the morning, we were expelled from the barrack. The Kapos were beating us again, but I no longer felt the pain. A glacial wind was enveloping us. We were naked, holding our shoes and belts. An order:

"Run!" And we ran. After a few minutes of running, a new barrack.

A barrel of foul-smelling liquid stood by the door. Disinfection. Everybody soaked in it. Then came a hot shower. All very fast. As we left the showers, we were chased outside. And ordered to run some more. Another barrack: the storeroom. Very long tables. Mountains of prison garb. As we ran, they threw the clothes at us: pants, jackets, shirts . . .

In a few seconds, we had ceased to be men. Had the situation not been so tragic, we might have laughed. We looked pretty strange! Meir Katz, a colossus, wore a child's pants, and Stern, a skinny little fellow, was floundering in a huge jacket. We immediately started to switch.

I glanced over at my father. How changed he looked! His eyes were veiled. I wanted to tell him something, but I didn't know what.

The night had passed completely. The morning star shone in the sky. I too had become a different person. The student of Talmud, the child I was, had been consumed by the flames. All that was left was a shape that resembled me. My soul had been invaded—and devoured—by a black flame.

So many events had taken place in just a few hours that I had completely lost all notion of time. When had we left our homes? And the ghetto? And the train? Only a week ago? One night? *One single night?*

How long had we been standing in the freezing wind? One hour? A single hour? Sixty minutes?

Surely it was a dream.

NOT FAR FROM US, prisoners were at work. Some were digging holes, others were carrying sand. None as much as glanced at us. We were withered trees in the heart of the desert. Behind me, people were talking. I had no desire to listen to what they were saying, or to know who was speaking and what about. Nobody dared raise his voice, even though there was no guard around. We whispered. Perhaps because of the thick smoke that poisoned the air and stung the throat.

We were herded into yet another barrack, inside the Gypsy camp. We fell into ranks of five.

"And now, stop moving!"

There was no floor. A roof and four walls. Our feet sank into the mud.

Again, the waiting. I fell asleep standing up. I dreamed of a bed, of my mother's hand on my face. I woke: I was standing, my feet in the mud. Some people collapsed, sliding into the mud. Others shouted:

"Are you crazy? We were told to stand. Do you want to get us all in trouble?"

As if all the troubles in the world were not already upon us.

Little by little, we all sat down in the mud. But we had to get up whenever a Kapo came in to check if, by chance, somebody had a new pair of shoes. If so, we had to hand them over. No use protesting; the blows multiplied and, in the end, one still had to hand them over.

I had new shoes myself. But as they were covered with a thick coat of mud, they had not been noticed. I thanked God, in an improvised prayer, for having created mud in His infinite and wondrous universe.

Suddenly, the silence became more oppressive. An SS officer had come in and, with him, the smell of the Angel of Death. We stared at his fleshy lips. He harangued us from the center of the barrack:

"You are in a concentration camp. In Auschwitz . . ."

A pause. He was observing the effect his words had produced. His face remains in my memory to this day. A tall man, in his thirties, crime written all over his forehead and his gaze. He looked at us as one would a pack of leprous dogs clinging to life.

"Remember," he went on. "Remember it always, let it be graven in your memories. You are in Auschwitz. And Auschwitz is not a convalescent home. It is a concentration camp. Here, you must work. If you don't you will go straight to the chimney. To the crematorium. Work or crematorium—the choice is yours."

We had already lived through a lot that night. We thought that nothing could frighten us anymore. But his harsh words sent shivers through us. The word "chimney" here was not an abstraction; it floated in the air, mingled with the smoke. It was, perhaps, the only word that had a real meaning in this place. He left the barrack. The Kapos arrived, shouting:

"All specialists—locksmiths, carpenters, electricians, watch-makers—one step forward!"

The rest of us were transferred to yet another barrack, this one of stone. We had permission to sit down. A Gypsy inmate was in charge.

My father suddenly had a colic attack. He got up and asked politely, in German:

"Excuse me . . . Could you tell me where the toilets are located?"

The Gypsy stared at him for a long time, from head to toe. As if he wished to ascertain that the person addressing him was actually a creature of flesh and bone, a human being with a body and a belly. Then, as if waking from a deep sleep, he slapped my father with such force that he fell down and then crawled back to his place on all fours.

I stood petrified. What had happened to me? My father had just been struck, in front of me, and I had not even blinked. I had watched and kept silent. Only yesterday, I would have dug my nails into this criminal's flesh. Had I changed that much? So fast? Remorse began to gnaw at me. All I could think was: I shall never forgive them for this. My father must have guessed my thoughts, because he whispered in my ear:

"It doesn't hurt." His cheek still bore the red mark of the hand.

"EVERYBODY OUTSIDE!"

A dozen or so Gypsies had come to join our guard. The clubs and whips were cracking around me. My feet were running on their own. I tried to protect myself from the blows by hiding behind others. It was spring. The sun was shining.

"Fall in, five by five!"

The prisoners I had glimpsed that morning were working nearby. No guard in sight, only the chimney's shadow . . . Lulled by the sunshine and my dreams, I felt someone pulling at my sleeve. It was my father: "Come on, son."

We marched. Gates opened and closed. We continued to march between the barbed wire. At every step, white signs with black skulls looked down on us. The inscription: WARNING! DANGER OF DEATH. What irony. Was there here a single place where one was *not* in danger of death?

The Gypsies had stopped next to a barrack. They were replaced by SS men, who encircled us with machine guns and police dogs.

The march had lasted half an hour. Looking around me, I noticed that the barbed wire was behind us. We had left the camp.

It was a beautiful day in May. The fragrances of spring were in the air. The sun was setting.

But no sooner had we taken a few more steps than we saw the barbed wire of another camp. This one had an iron gate with the overhead inscription: ARBEIT MACHT FREI. Work makes you free.

Auschwitz.

FIRST IMPRESSION: better than Birkenau. Cement buildings with two stories rather than wooden barracks. Little gardens here and there. We were led toward one of those "blocks." Seated on the ground by the entrance, we began to wait again. From time to time somebody was allowed to go in. These were the showers, a compulsory routine. Going from one camp to the other, several times a day, we had, each time, to go through them.

40

After the hot shower, we stood shivering in the darkness. Our clothes had been left behind; we had been promised other clothes.

Around midnight, we were told to run.

"Faster!" yelled our guards. "The faster you run, the faster you'll get to go to sleep."

After a few minutes of racing madly, we came to a new block. The man in charge was waiting. He was a young Pole, who was smiling at us. He began to talk to us and, despite our weariness, we listened attentively.

"Comrades, you are now in the concentration camp Auschwitz. Ahead of you lies a long road paved with suffering. Don't lose hope. You have already eluded the worst danger: the selection. Therefore, muster your strength and keep your faith. We shall all see the day of liberation. Have faith in life, a thousand times faith. By driving out despair, you will move away from death. Hell does not last forever . . . And now, here is a prayer, or rather a piece of advice: let there be camaraderie among you. We are all brothers and share the same fate. The same smoke hovers over all our heads. Help each other. That is the only way to survive. And now, enough said, you are tired. Listen: you are in Block 17; I am responsible for keeping order here. Anyone with a complaint may come to see me. That is all. Go to sleep. Two people to a bunk. Good night."

Those were the first human words.

NO SOONER HAD WE CLIMBED into our bunks than we fell into a deep sleep.

The next morning, the "veteran" inmates treated us without brutality. We went to wash. We were given new clothing. They brought us black coffee.

We left the block around ten o'clock, so it could be cleaned.

Outside, the sun warmed us. Our morale was much improved. A good night's sleep had done its work. Friends met, exchanged a few sentences. We spoke of everything without ever mentioning those who had disappeared. The prevailing opinion was that the war was about to end.

At about noon, we were brought some soup, one bowl of thick soup for each of us. I was terribly hungry, yet I refused to touch it. I was still the spoiled child of long ago. My father swallowed my ration.

We then had a short nap in the shade of the block. That SS officer in the muddy barrack must have been lying: Auschwitz was, after all, a convalescent home . . .

In the afternoon, they made us line up. Three prisoners brought a table and some medical instruments. We were told to roll up our left sleeves and file past the table. The three "veteran" prisoners, needles in hand, tattooed numbers on our left arms. I became A-7713. From then on, I had no other name.

At dusk, a roll call. The work Kommandos had returned. The orchestra played military marches near the camp entrance. Tens of thousands of inmates stood in rows while the SS checked their numbers.

After the roll call, the prisoners from all the blocks dispersed, looking for friends, relatives, or neighbors among the arrivals of the latest convoy.

DAYS WENT BY. In the mornings: black coffee. At midday: soup. By the third day, I was eagerly eating any kind of soup . . . At six o'clock in the afternoon: roll call. Followed by bread with something. At nine o'clock: bedtime.

We had already been in Auschwitz for eight days. It was after roll call. We stood waiting for the bell announcing its end. Suddenly I noticed someone passing between the rows. I heard him ask:

"Who among you is Wiesel from Sighet?"

The person looking for us was a small fellow with spectacles in a wizened face. My father answered:

"That's me. Wiesel from Sighet."

The fellow's eyes narrowed. He took a long look at my father.

"You don't know me? . . . You don't recognize me. I'm your relative, Stein. Already forgotten? Stein. Stein from Antwerp. Reizel's husband. Your wife was Reizel's aunt . . . She often wrote to us . . . and such letters!"

My father had not recognized him. He must have barely known him, always being up to his neck in communal affairs and not knowledgeable in family matters. He was always elsewhere, lost in thought. (Once, a cousin came to see us in Sighet. She had stayed at our house and eaten at our table for two weeks before my father noticed her presence for the first time.) No, he did not remember Stein. I recognized him right away. I had known Reizel, his wife, before she had left for Belgium.

He told us that he had been deported in 1942. He said, "I heard people say that a transport had arrived from your region and I came to look for you. I thought you might have some news of Reizel and my two small boys, who stayed in Antwerp . . ."

I knew nothing about them . . . Since 1940, my mother had not received a single letter from them. But I lied:

"Yes, my mother did hear from them. Reizel is fine. So are the children . . ."

He was weeping with joy. He would have liked to stay longer, to learn more details, to soak up the good news, but an SS was heading in our direction and he had to go, telling us that he would come back the next day.

The bell announced that we were dismissed. We went to fetch the evening meal: bread and margarine. I was terribly hungry and swallowed my ration on the spot. My father told me, "You mustn't eat all at once. Tomorrow is another day . . ."

But seeing that his advice had come too late, and that there was nothing left of my ration, he didn't even start his own.

"Me, I'm not hungry," he said.

WE REMAINED IN AUSCHWITZ for three weeks. We had nothing to do. We slept a lot. In the afternoon and at night.

Our one goal was to avoid the transports, to stay here as long as possible. It wasn't difficult; it was enough never to sign up as a skilled worker. The unskilled workers were kept until the end.

At the start of the third week, our *Blockälteste* was removed; he was judged too humane. The new one was ferocious and his aides were veritable monsters. The good days were over. We began to wonder whether it wouldn't be better to let ourselves be chosen for the next transport.

Stein, our relative from Antwerp, continued to visit us and, from time to time, he would bring a half portion of bread:

"Here, this is for you, Eliezer."

Every time he came, tears would roll down his icy cheeks. He would often say to my father:

"Take care of your son. He is very weak, very dehydrated. Take care of yourselves, you must avoid selection. Eat! Anything, anytime. Eat all you can. The weak don't last very long around here . . ."

And he himself was so thin, so withered, so weak . . .

"The only thing that keeps me alive," he kept saying, "is to know that Reizel and the little ones are still alive. Were it not for them, I would give up."

One evening, he came to see us, his face radiant.

"A transport just arrived from Antwerp. I shall go to see them tomorrow. Surely they will have news . . ."

He left.

We never saw him again. He had been given the news. The *real* news.

EVENINGS, AS WE LAY on our cots, we sometimes tried to sing a few Hasidic melodies. Akiba Drumer would break our hearts with his deep, grave voice.

Some of the men spoke of God: His mysterious ways, the sins of the Jewish people, and the redemption to come. As for me, I had ceased to pray. I concurred with Job! I was not denying His existence, but I doubted His absolute justice.

Akiba Drumer said:

"God is testing us. He wants to see whether we are capable of overcoming our base instincts, of killing the Satan within ourselves. We have no right to despair. And if He punishes us mercilessly, it is a sign that He loves us that much more . . ."

Hersh Genud, well versed in Kabbalah, spoke of the end of the world and the coming of the Messiah.

From time to time, in the middle of all that talk, a thought buzzed in my mind: "Where is Mother right now . . . and Tzipora . . ."

"Mother is still a young woman," my father once said. "She must be in a labor camp. And Tzipora, she is a big girl now. She too must be in a camp . . ."

How we would have liked to believe that. We pretended, for what if one of us still *did* believe?

ALL THE SKILLED WORKERS had already been sent to other camps. Only about a hundred of us, simple laborers, were left.

"Today, it's your turn," announced the block secretary. "You are leaving with the next transport."

At ten o'clock, we were handed our daily ration of bread. A dozen or so SS surrounded us. At the gate, the sign proclaimed that work meant freedom. We were counted. And there we were, in the countryside, on a sunny road. In the sky, a few small white clouds.

We were walking slowly. The guards were in no hurry. We were glad of it. As we were passing through some of the villages, many Germans watched us, showing no surprise. No doubt they had seen quite a few of these processions . . .

On the way, we saw some young German girls. The guards began to tease them. The girls giggled. They allowed themselves to be kissed and tickled, bursting with laughter. They all were laughing, joking, and passing love notes to one another. At least, during all that time, we endured neither shouting nor blows.

After four hours, we arrived at the new camp: Buna. The iron gate closed behind us.

THE CAMP looked as though it had been through an epidemic: empty and dead. Only a few "well-dressed" inmates were wandering between the blocks.

Of course, we first had to pass through the showers. The head of the camp joined us there. He was a stocky man with big shoulders, the neck of a bull, thick lips, and curly hair. He gave an impression of kindness. From time to time, a smile would linger in his gray-blue eyes. Our convoy included a few ten- and twelve-year-olds. The officer took an interest in them and gave orders to bring them food.

We were given new clothing and settled in two tents. We were to wait there until we could be incorporated into work Kommandos. Then we would be assigned to a block.

In the evening, the Kommandos returned from the work yards. Roll call. We began looking for people we knew, asking the "veterans" which work Kommandos were the best and which block one should try to enter. All the inmates agreed:

"Buna is a very good camp. One can hold one's own here. The most important thing is not to be assigned to the construction Kommando . . ."

As if we had a choice . . .

Our tent leader was a German. An assassin's face, fleshy lips, hands resembling a wolf's paws. The camp's food had agreed with him; he could hardly move, he was so fat. Like the head of the camp, he liked children. Immediately after our arrival, he had bread brought for them, some soup and margarine. (In fact, this affection was not entirely altruistic; there existed here a veritable traffic of children among homosexuals, I learned later.) He told us:

"You will stay with me for three days in quarantine. Afterward, you will go to work. Tomorrow: medical checkup."

One of his aides—a tough-looking boy with shifty eyes—came over to me:

"Would you like to get into a good Kommando?"

"Of course. But on one condition: I want to stay with my father."

"All right," he said. "I can arrange it. For a pittance: your shoes. I'll give you another pair."

I refused to give him my shoes. They were all I had left.

"I'll also give you a ration of bread with some margarine . . ."

He liked my shoes; I would not let him have them. Later, they were taken from me anyway. In exchange for nothing, that time.

The medical checkup took place outside, early in the morning, before three doctors seated on a bench.

The first hardly examined me. He just asked:

"Are you in good health?"

Who would have dared to admit the opposite?

On the other hand, the dentist seemed more conscientious: he asked me to open my mouth wide. In fact, he was not looking for decay but for gold teeth. Those who had gold in their mouths were listed by their number. I did have a gold crown.

The first three days went by quickly. On the fourth day, as we stood in front of our tent, the Kapos appeared. Each one began to choose the men he liked:

"You . . . you . . . you . . ." They pointed their fingers, the way one might choose cattle, or merchandise.

We followed our Kapo, a young man. He made us halt at the door of the first block, near the entrance to the camp. This was the orchestra's block. He motioned us inside. We were surprised; what had we to do with music?

The orchestra was playing a military march, always the same. Dozens of Kommandos were marching off, in step, to the work yards. The Kapos were beating the time:

"Left, right, left, right."

SS officers, pen in hand, recorded the number of men leaving. The orchestra continued to play the same march until the last Kommando had passed. Then the conductor's baton stopped moving and the orchestra fell silent. The Kapo yelled:

"Fall in!"

We fell into ranks of five, with the musicians. We left the camp without music but in step. We still had the march in our ears.

"Left, right, left, right!"

We struck up conversations with our neighbors, the musicians. Almost all of them were Jews. Juliek, a Pole with eyeglasses and a cynical smile in a pale face. Louis, a native of Holland, a well-known violinist. He complained that they would not let him play Beethoven; Jews were not allowed to play German music. Hans, the young man from Berlin, was full of wit. The foreman was a Pole: Franek, a former student in Warsaw.

Juliek explained to me, "We work in a warehouse of electrical materials, not far from here. The work is neither difficult nor dangerous. Only Idek, the Kapo, occasionally has fits of madness, and then you'd better stay out of his way."

"You are lucky, little fellow," said Hans, smiling. "You fell into a good Kommando . . ."

Ten minutes later, we stood in front of the warehouse. A German employee, a civilian, the *Meister*, came to meet us. He paid as much attention to us as would a shopkeeper receiving a delivery of old rags.

Our comrades were right. The work was not difficult. Sitting on the ground, we counted bolts, bulbs, and various small electrical parts. The Kapo launched into a lengthy explanation of the importance of this work, warning us that anyone who proved to be lazy would be held accountable. My new comrades reassured me:

"Don't worry. He has to say this because of the *Meister*."

There were many Polish civilians here and a few Frenchwomen as well. The women silently greeted the musicians with their eyes.

Franek, the foreman, assigned me to a corner:

"Don't kill yourself. There's no hurry. But watch out. Don't let an SS catch you."

"Please, sir . . . I'd like to be near my father."

"All right. Your father will work here, next to you."

We were lucky.

Two boys came to join our group: Yossi and Tibi, two brothers from Czechoslovakia whose parents had been exterminated in Birkenau. They lived for each other, body and soul.

They quickly became my friends. Having once belonged to a Zionist youth organization, they knew countless Hebrew songs. And so we would sometimes hum melodies evoking the gentle waters of the Jordan River and the majestic sanctity of Jerusalem. We also spoke often about Palestine. Their parents, like mine, had not had the courage to sell everything and emigrate while there was still time. We decided that if we were allowed to live until the Liberation, we would not stay another day in Europe. We would board the first ship to Haifa.

Still lost in his Kabbalistic dreams, Akiba Drumer had discovered a verse from the Bible that, translated into numbers, made it possible for him to predict redemption in the weeks to come.

WE HAD LEFT THE TENTS for the musicians' block. We now were entitled to a blanket, a washbowl, and a bar of soap. The *Blockälteste* was a German Jew.

It was good to have a Jew as your leader. His name was Alphonse. A young man with a startlingly wizened face. He was totally devoted to defending "his" block. Whenever he could, he would "organize" a cauldron of soup for the young, the weak, for all those who dreamed more of an extra portion of food than of liberty.

ONE DAY, when we had just returned from the warehouse, I was summoned by the block secretary:

"A-7713?"

"That's me."

"After your meal, you'll go to see the dentist."

"But . . . I don't have a toothache . . ."

"After your meal. Without fail."

I went to the infirmary block. Some twenty prisoners were waiting in line at the entrance. It didn't take long to learn the reason for our summons: our gold teeth were to be extracted.

The dentist, a Jew from Czechoslovakia, had a face not unlike a death mask. When he opened his mouth, one had a ghastly vision of yellow, rotten teeth. Seated in the chair, I asked meekly:

"What are you going to do, sir?"

"I shall remove your gold crown, that's all," he said, clearly indifferent.

I thought of pretending to be sick:

"Couldn't you wait a few days, sir? I don't feel well, I have a fever . . ."

He wrinkled his brow, thought for a moment, and took my pulse.

"All right, son. Come back to see me when you feel better. But don't wait for me to call you!"

I went back to see him a week later. With the same excuse: I still was not feeling better. He did not seem surprised, and I don't know whether he believed me. Yet he most likely was pleased that I had come back on my own, as I had promised. He granted me a further delay.

A few days after my visit, the dentist's office was shut down. He had been thrown into prison and was about to be hanged. It appeared that he had been dealing in the prisoners' gold teeth for his own benefit. I felt no pity for him. In fact, I was pleased with what was happening to him: my gold crown was safe. It could be useful to me one day, to buy something, some bread or even time to live. At that moment in time, all that mattered to me was my daily bowl of soup, my crust of stale bread. The bread, the soup—those were my entire life. I was nothing but a body. Perhaps even less: a famished stomach. The stomach alone was measuring time.

IN THE WAREHOUSE, I often worked next to a young Frenchwoman. We did not speak: she did not know German and I did not understand French.

I thought she looked Jewish, though she passed for "Aryan." She was a forced labor inmate.

One day when Idek was venting his fury, I happened to cross his path. He threw himself on me like a wild beast, beating me in the chest, on my head, throwing me to the ground and picking me up again, crushing me with ever more violent blows, until I was covered in blood. As I bit my lips in order not to howl with pain, he must have mistaken my silence for defiance and so he continued to hit me harder and harder.

Abruptly, he calmed down and sent me back to work as if nothing had happened. As if we had taken part in a game in which both roles were of equal importance.

I dragged myself to my corner. I was aching all over. I felt a cool hand wiping the blood from my forehead. It was the French girl. She was smiling her mournful smile as she slipped me a crust of bread. She looked straight into my eyes. I knew she wanted to talk to me but that she was paralyzed with fear. She remained like that for some time, and then her face lit up and she said, in almost perfect German:

"Bite your lips, little brother . . . Don't cry. Keep your anger, your hate, for another day, for later. The day will come but not now . . . Wait. Clench your teeth and wait . . ."

MANY YEARS LATER, in Paris, I sat in the Métro, reading my newspaper. Across the aisle, a beautiful woman with dark hair and dreamy eyes. I had seen those eyes before.

"Madame, don't you recognize me?"

"I don't know you, sir."

"In 1944, you were in Poland, in Buna, weren't you?"

"Yes, but . . ."

"You worked in a depot, a warehouse for electrical parts . . ."

"Yes," she said, looking troubled. And then, after a moment of silence: "Wait . . . I do remember . . ."

"Idek, the Kapo . . . the young Jewish boy . . . your sweet words . . ."

We left the Métro together and sat down at a café terrace. We spent the whole evening reminiscing. Before we parted, I said, "May I ask one more question?"

"I know what it is: Am I Jewish . . . ? Yes, I am. From an observant family. During the Occupation, I had false papers and passed as Aryan. And that was how I was assigned to a forced labor unit.

When they deported me to Germany, I eluded being sent to a concentration camp. At the depot, nobody knew that I spoke German; it would have aroused suspicion. It was imprudent of me to say those few words to you, but I knew that you would not betray me . . ."

ANOTHER TIME we were loading diesel motors onto freight cars under the supervision of some German soldiers. Idek was on edge, he had trouble restraining himself. Suddenly, he exploded. The victim this time was my father.

"You old loafer!" he started yelling. "Is this what you call working?"

And he began beating him with an iron bar. At first, my father simply doubled over under the blows, but then he seemed to break in two like an old tree struck by lightning.

I had watched it all happening without moving. I kept silent. In fact, I thought of stealing away in order not to suffer the blows. What's more, if I felt anger at that moment, it was not directed at the Kapo but at my father. Why couldn't he have avoided Idek's wrath? That was what life in a concentration camp had made of me . . .

Franek, the foreman, one day noticed the gold crown in my mouth:

"Let me have your crown, kid."

I answered that I could not, because without that crown I could no longer eat.

"For what they give you to eat, kid . . ."

I found another answer: my crown had been listed in the register during the medical checkup; this could mean trouble for us both.

"If you don't give me your crown, it will cost you much more!"

All of a sudden, this pleasant and intelligent young man had changed. His eyes were shining with greed. I told him that I needed to get my father's advice.

"Go ahead, kid, ask. But I want the answer by tomorrow."

When I mentioned it to my father, he hesitated. After a long silence, he said:

"No, my son. We cannot do this."

"He will seek revenge!"

"He won't dare, my son."

Unfortunately, Franek knew how to handle this; he knew my weak spot. My father had never served in the military and could not march in step. But here, whenever we moved from one place to another, it was in step. That presented Franek with the opportunity to torment him and, on a daily basis, to thrash him savagely. Left, right: he punched him. Left, right: he slapped him.

I decided to give my father lessons in marching in step, in keeping time. We began practicing in front of our block. I would command: "Left, right!" and my father would try. The inmates made fun of us: "Look at the little officer, teaching the old man to march . . . Hey, little general, how many rations of bread does the old man give you for this?"

But my father did not make sufficient progress, and the blows continued to rain on him.

"So! You still don't know how to march in step, you old good-for-nothing?"

This went on for two weeks. It was untenable. We had to give in. That day, Franek burst into savage laughter:

"I knew it, I knew that I would win, kid. Better late than never. And because you made me wait, it will also cost you a ration of bread. A ration of bread for one of my pals, a famous dentist from Warsaw. To pay him for pulling out your crown."

"What? My ration of bread so that you can have *my* crown?"

Franek smiled.

"What would you like? That I break your teeth by smashing your face?"

That evening, in the latrines, the dentist from Warsaw pulled my crown with the help of a rusty spoon.

Franek became pleasant again. From time to time, he even gave me extra soup. But it didn't last long. Two weeks later, all the Poles were transferred to another camp. I had lost my crown for nothing.

A FEW DAYS BEFORE the Poles left, I had a novel experience.

It was on a Sunday morning. Our Kommando was not required to work that day. Only Idek would not hear of staying in the camp. We had to go to the depot. This sudden enthusiasm for work astonished us. At the depot, Idek entrusted us to Franek, saying, "Do what you like. But do something. Or else, you'll hear from me . . ."

And he disappeared.

We didn't know what to do. Tired of huddling on the ground, we each took turns strolling through the warehouse, in the hope of finding something, a piece of bread, perhaps, that a civilian might have forgotten there.

When I reached the back of the building, I heard sounds coming from a small adjoining room. I moved closer and had a glimpse of Idek and a young Polish girl, half naked, on a straw mat. Now I understood why Idek refused to leave us in the camp. He moved one hundred prisoners so that he could copulate with this girl! It struck me as terribly funny and I burst out laughing.

Idek jumped, turned, and saw me, while the girl tried to cover her breasts. I wanted to run away, but my feet were nailed to the floor. Idek grabbed me by the throat.

Hissing at me, he threatened:

"Just you wait, kid . . . You will see what it costs to leave your work . . . You'll pay for this later . . . And now go back to your place . . ."

A HALF HOUR BEFORE the usual time to stop work, the Kapo assembled the entire Kommando. Roll call. Nobody understood what was going on. A roll call at this hour? Here? Only I knew. The Kapo made a short speech:

"An ordinary inmate does not have the right to mix into other people's affairs. One of you does not seem to have understood this point. I shall therefore try to make him understand clearly, once and for all."

I felt the sweat running down my back.

"A-7713!"

I stepped forward.

"A crate!" he ordered.

They brought a crate.

"Lie down on it! On your belly!"

I obeyed.

I no longer felt anything except the lashes of the whip.

"One! . . . Two! . . ." he was counting.

He took his time between lashes. Only the first really hurt. I heard him count:

"Ten . . . eleven! . . ."

His voice was calm and reached me as through a thick wall.

"Twenty-three . . ."

Two more, I thought, half unconscious.

The Kapo was waiting.

"Twenty-four . . . twenty-five!"

It was over. I had not realized it, but I had fainted. I came to when they doused me with cold water. I was still lying on the crate. In a blur, I could see the wet ground next to me. Then I heard someone yell. It had to be the Kapo. I began to distinguish what he was shouting:

"Stand up!"

I must have made some movement to get up, but I felt myself fall back on the crate. How I wanted to get up!

"Stand up!" He was yelling even more loudly.

If only I could answer him, if only I could tell him that I could not move. But my mouth would not open.

At Idek's command, two inmates lifted me and led me to him.

"Look me in the eye!"

I looked at him without seeing him. I was thinking of my father. He would be suffering more than I.

"Listen to me, you son of a swine!" said Idek coldly. "So much for your curiosity. You shall receive five times more if you dare tell anyone what you saw! Understood?"

I nodded, once, ten times, endlessly. As if my head had decided to say yes for all eternity.

ONE SUNDAY, as half of our group, including my father, was at work, the others, including me, took the opportunity to stay and rest.

At around ten o'clock, the sirens started to go off. Alert. The *Blockälteste* gathered us inside the blocks, while the SS took refuge in the shelters. As it was relatively easy to escape during an alert— the guards left the watchtowers, and the electric current in the barbed wire was cut—the standing order to the SS was to shoot anyone found outside his block.

In no time, the camp had the look of an abandoned ship. No living soul in the alleys. Next to the kitchen, two cauldrons of hot, steaming soup had been left untended. Two cauldrons of soup! Smack in the middle of the road, two cauldrons of soup with no one to guard them! A royal feast going to waste! Supreme temptation! Hundreds of eyes were looking at them, shining with desire. Two lambs with hundreds of wolves lying in wait for them. Two lambs without a shepherd, free for the taking. But who would dare?

Fear was greater than hunger. Suddenly, we saw the door of Block 37 open slightly. A man appeared, crawling snakelike in the direction of the cauldrons.

Hundreds of eyes were watching his every move. Hundreds of men were crawling with him, scraping their bodies with his on the stones. All hearts trembled, but mostly with envy. He was the one who had dared.

He reached the first cauldron. Hearts were pounding harder: he had succeeded. Jealousy devoured us, consumed us. We never thought to admire him. Poor hero committing suicide for a ration or two or more of soup . . . In our minds, he was already dead.

Lying on the ground near the cauldron, he was trying to lift himself to the cauldron's rim. Either out of weakness or out of fear, he remained there, undoubtedly to muster his strength. At last he succeeded in pulling himself up to the rim. For a second, he seemed to be looking at himself in the soup, looking for his ghostly reflection there. Then, for no apparent reason, he let out a terrible scream, a death rattle such as I had never heard before, and, with open mouth, thrust his head toward the still steaming liquid. We jumped at the sound of the shot. Falling to the ground, his face stained by the soup, the man writhed a few seconds at the base of the cauldron, and then he was still.

That was when we began to hear the planes. Almost at the same moment, the barrack began to shake.

"They're bombing the Buna factory," someone shouted.

I anxiously thought of my father, who was at work. But I was glad nevertheless. To watch that factory go up in flames—what revenge! While we had heard some talk of German military defeats on the various fronts, we were not sure if they were credible. But today, this was real!

We were not afraid. And yet, if a bomb had fallen on the blocks, it would have claimed hundreds of inmates' lives. But we no longer feared death, in any event not this particular death. Every bomb that hit filled us with joy, gave us renewed confidence.

The raid lasted more than one hour. If only it could have gone on for ten times ten hours . . . Then, once more, there was silence. The last sound of the American plane dissipated in the wind and there we were, in our cemetery. On the horizon we saw a long trail of black smoke. The sirens began to wail again. The end of the alert.

Everyone came out of the blocks. We breathed in air filled with fire and smoke, and our eyes shone with hope. A bomb had landed in the middle of the camp, near the *Appelplatz*, the assembly point, but had not exploded. We had to dispose of it outside the camp.

The head of the camp, the *Lagerälteste*, accompanied by his aide and by the chief Kapo, were on an inspection tour of the camp. The raid had left traces of great fear on his face.

In the very center of the camp lay the body of the man with soup stains on his face, the only victim. The cauldrons were carried back to the kitchen.

The SS were back at their posts in the watchtowers, behind their machine guns. Intermission was over.

An hour later, we saw the Kommandos returning, in step as always. Happily, I caught sight of my father.

"Several buildings were flattened," he said, "but the depot was not touched . . ."

In the afternoon, we cheerfully went to clear the ruins.

ONE WEEK LATER, as we returned from work, there, in the middle of the camp, in the *Appelplatz*, stood a black gallows.

We learned that soup would be distributed only after roll call, which lasted longer than usual. The orders were given more harshly than on other days, and there were strange vibrations in the air.

"Caps off!" the *Lagerälteste* suddenly shouted.

Ten thousand caps came off at once.

"Cover your heads!"

Ten thousand caps were back on our heads, at lightning speed.

The camp gate opened. An SS unit appeared and encircled us: one SS every three paces. The machine guns on the watchtowers were pointed toward the *Appelplatz*.

"They're expecting trouble," whispered Juliek.

Two SS were headed toward the solitary confinement cell. They came back, the condemned man between them. He was a young boy from Warsaw. An inmate with three years in concentration camps behind him. He was tall and strong, a giant compared to me.

His back was to the gallows, his face turned toward his judge, the head of the camp. He was pale but seemed more solemn than frightened. His manacled hands did not tremble. His eyes were coolly assessing the hundreds of SS guards, the thousands of prisoners surrounding him.

The *Lagerälteste* began to read the verdict, emphasizing every word:

"In the name of Reichsführer Himmler . . . prisoner number . . . stole during the air raid . . . according to the law . . . prisoner number . . . is condemned to death. Let this be a warning and an example to all prisoners."

Nobody moved.

I heard the pounding of my heart. The thousands of people who died daily in Auschwitz and Birkenau, in the crematoria, no longer troubled me. But this boy, leaning against his gallows, upset me deeply.

"This ceremony, will it be over soon? I'm hungry . . ." whispered Juliek.

At a sign of the *Lagerälteste*, the *Lagerkapo* stepped up to the condemned youth. He was assisted by two prisoners. In exchange for two bowls of soup.

The Kapo wanted to blindfold the youth, but he refused.

After what seemed like a long moment, the hangman put the rope around his neck. He was about to signal his aides to pull the chair from under the young man's feet when the latter shouted, in a strong and calm voice:

"Long live liberty! My curse on Germany! My curse! My—"

The executioner had completed his work.

Like a sword, the order cut through the air:

"Caps off!"

Ten thousand prisoners paid their respects.

"Cover your heads!"

Then the entire camp, block after block, filed past the hanged boy and stared at his extinguished eyes, the tongue hanging from his gaping mouth. The Kapos forced everyone to look him squarely in the face.

Afterward, we were given permission to go back to our block and have our meal.

I remember that on that evening, the soup tasted better than ever . . .

I WATCHED OTHER HANGINGS. I never saw a single victim weep. These withered bodies had long forgotten the bitter taste of tears.

Except once. The *Oberkapo* of the Fifty-second Cable Kommando was a Dutchman: a giant of a man, well over six feet. He had some seven hundred prisoners under his command, and they all loved him like a brother. Nobody had ever endured a blow or even an insult from him.

In his "service" was a young boy, a *pipel*, as they were called. A child with a delicate and beautiful face—an incredible sight in this camp.

(In Buna, the *pipel* were hated; they often displayed greater cruelty than their elders. I once saw one of them, a boy of thirteen, beat his father for not making his bed properly. As the old man quietly wept, the boy was yelling: "If you don't stop crying instantly, I will no longer bring you bread. Understood?" But the Dutchman's little servant was beloved by all. His was the face of an angel in distress.)

One day the power failed at the central electric plant in Buna. The Gestapo, summoned to inspect the damage, concluded that it was sabotage. They found a trail. It led to the block of the Dutch *Oberkapo*. And after a search, they found a significant quantity of weapons.

The *Oberkapo* was arrested on the spot. He was tortured for weeks on end, in vain. He gave no names. He was transferred to Auschwitz. And never heard from again.

But his young *pipel* remained behind, in solitary confinement. He too was tortured, but he too remained silent. The SS then condemned him to death, him and two other inmates who had been found to possess arms.

One day, as we returned from work, we saw three gallows, three black ravens, erected on the *Appelplatz*. Roll call. The SS surrounding us, machine guns aimed at us: the usual ritual. Three prisoners in chains—and, among them, the little *pipel*, the sad-eyed angel.

The SS seemed more preoccupied, more worried, than usual. To hang a child in front of thousands of onlookers was not a small matter. The head of the camp read the verdict. All eyes were on the child. He was pale, almost calm, but he was biting his lips as he stood in the shadow of the gallows.

This time, the *Lagerkapo* refused to act as executioner. Three SS took his place.

The three condemned prisoners together stepped onto the chairs. In unison, the nooses were placed around their necks.

"Long live liberty!" shouted the two men.

But the boy was silent.

"Where is merciful God, where is He?" someone behind me was asking.

At the signal, the three chairs were tipped over.

Total silence in the camp. On the horizon, the sun was setting.

"Caps off!" screamed the *Lagerälteste*. His voice quivered. As for the rest of us, we were weeping.

"Cover your heads!"

Then came the march past the victims. The two men were no longer alive. Their tongues were hanging out, swollen and bluish. But the third rope was still moving: the child, too light, was still breathing . . .

And so he remained for more than half an hour, lingering between life and death, writhing before our eyes. And we were forced to look at him at close range. He was still alive when I passed him. His tongue was still red, his eyes not yet extinguished.

Behind me, I heard the same man asking:

"For God's sake, where is God?"

And from within me, I heard a voice answer:

"Where is He? This is where—hanging here from this gallows . . ."

That night, the soup tasted of corpses.

THE SUMMER WAS COMING TO AN END. The Jewish year was almost over. On the eve of Rosh Hashanah, the last day of that cursed year, the entire camp was agitated and every one of us felt the tension. After all, this was a day unlike all others. The last day of the year. The word "last" had an odd ring to it. What if it really were the last day?

The evening meal was distributed, an especially thick soup, but nobody touched it. We wanted to wait until after prayer. On the *Appelplatz*, surrounded by electrified barbed wire, thousands of Jews, anguish on their faces, gathered in silence.

Night was falling rapidly. And more and more prisoners kept coming, from every block, suddenly able to overcome time and space, to will both into submission.

What are You, my God? I thought angrily. How do You compare to this stricken mass gathered to affirm to You their faith, their anger, their defiance? What does Your grandeur mean, Master of the Universe, in the face of all this cowardice, this decay, and this misery? Why do You go on troubling these poor people's wounded minds, their ailing bodies?

SOME TEN THOUSAND MEN had come to participate in a solemn service, including the *Blockälteste*, the Kapos, all bureaucrats in the service of Death.

"Blessed be the Almighty . . ."

The voice of the officiating inmate had just become audible. At first I thought it was the wind.

"Blessed be God's name . . ."

Thousands of lips repeated the benediction, bent over like trees in a storm.

Blessed be God's name?

Why, but why would I bless Him? Every fiber in me rebelled. Because He caused thousands of children to burn in His mass graves? Because He kept six crematoria working day and night, including Sabbath and the Holy Days? Because, in His great might, He had created Auschwitz, Birkenau, Buna, and so many other factories of death? How could I say to Him: Blessed be Thou, Almighty, Master of the Universe, who chose us among all nations to be tortured day and night, to watch as our fathers, our mothers, our brothers end up in the furnaces? Praised be Thy Holy Name, for having chosen us to be slaughtered on Thine altar?

I listened as the inmate's voice rose; it was powerful yet broken, amid the weeping, the sobbing, the sighing of the entire "congregation":

"All the earth and universe are God's!"

He kept pausing, as though he lacked the strength to uncover the meaning beneath the text. The melody was stifled in his throat.

And I, the former mystic, was thinking: Yes, man is stronger, greater than God. When Adam and Eve deceived You, You chased them from paradise. When You were displeased by Noah's generation, You brought down the Flood. When Sodom lost Your favor,

You caused the heavens to rain down fire and damnation. But look at these men whom You have betrayed, allowing them to be tortured, slaughtered, gassed, and burned, what do they do? They pray before You! They praise Your name!

"All of creation bears witness to the Greatness of God!"

In days gone by, Rosh Hashanah had dominated my life. I knew that my sins grieved the Almighty and so I pleaded for forgiveness. In those days, I fully believed that the salvation of the world depended on every one of my deeds, on every one of my prayers.

But now, I no longer pleaded for anything. I was no longer able to lament. On the contrary, I felt very strong. I was the accuser, God the accused. My eyes had opened and I was alone, terribly alone in a world without God, without man. Without love or mercy. I was nothing but ashes now, but I felt myself to be stronger than this Almighty to whom my life had been bound for so long. In the midst of these men assembled for prayer, I felt like an observer, a stranger.

The service ended with Kaddish. Each one recited Kaddish for his parents, for his children, and for himself.

We remained standing in the *Appelplatz* for a long time, unable to detach ourselves from this surreal moment. Then came the time to go to sleep, and slowly the inmates returned to their blocks. I thought I heard them wishing each other a Happy New Year!

I ran to look for my father. At the same time I was afraid of having to wish him a happy year in which I no longer believed. He was leaning against the wall, bent shoulders sagging as if under a heavy load. I went up to him, took his hand, and kissed it. I felt a tear on my hand. Whose was it? Mine? His? I said nothing. Nor did he. Never before had we understood each other so clearly.

The sound of the bell brought us back to reality. We had to go to bed. We came back from very far away. I looked up at my father's face, trying to glimpse a smile or something like it on his stricken face. But there was nothing. Not the shadow of an expression. Defeat.

YOM KIPPUR. The Day of Atonement. Should we fast? The question was hotly debated. To fast could mean a more certain, more rapid death. In this place, we were always fasting. It was Yom Kippur year-round. But there were those who said we should fast, precisely because it was dangerous to do so. We needed to show God that even here, locked in hell, we were capable of singing His praises.

I did not fast. First of all, to please my father, who had forbidden me to do so. And then, there was no longer any reason for me to fast. I no longer accepted God's silence. As I swallowed my ration of soup, I turned that act into a symbol of rebellion, of protest against Him.

And I nibbled on my crust of bread.

Deep inside me, I felt a great void opening.

THE SS OFFERED us a beautiful present for the new year.

We had just returned from work. As soon as we passed the camp's entrance, we sensed something out of the ordinary in the air. The roll call was shorter than usual. The evening soup was distributed at great speed, swallowed as quickly. We were anxious.

I was no longer in the same block as my father. They had transferred me to another Kommando, the construction one, where twelve hours a day I hauled heavy slabs of stone. The head of my new block was a German Jew, small with piercing eyes. That evening he announced to us that henceforth no one was allowed to leave the block after the evening soup. A terrible word began to circulate soon thereafter: selection.

We knew what it meant. An SS would examine us. Whenever he found someone extremely frail—a "Muselman" was what we called those inmates—he would write down his number: good for the crematorium.

After the soup, we gathered between the bunks. The veterans told us: "You're lucky to have been brought here so late. Today, this is paradise compared to what the camp was two years ago. Back then, Buna was a veritable hell. No water, no blankets, less soup and bread. At night, we slept almost naked and the temperature was thirty below. We were collecting corpses by the hundreds every day. Work was very hard. Today, this is a little paradise. The Kapos back then had orders to kill a certain number of prisoners every day. And every week, selection. A merciless selection . . . Yes, you are lucky."

"Enough! Be quiet!" I begged them. "Tell your stories tomorrow, or some other day."

They burst out laughing. They were not veterans for nothing.

"Are you scared? We too were scared. And, at that time, for good reason."

The old men stayed in their corner, silent, motionless, hunted-down creatures. Some were praying.

One more hour. Then we would know the verdict: death or reprieve.

And my father? I first thought of him now. How would he pass selection? He had aged so much . . .

Our *Blockälteste* had not been outside a concentration camp since 1933. He had already been through all the slaughterhouses, all the factories of death. Around nine o'clock, he came to stand in our midst:

"*Achtung!*"

There was instant silence.

"Listen carefully to what I am about to tell you." For the first time, his voice quivered. "In a few moments, selection will take place. You will have to undress completely. Then you will go, one by one, before the SS doctors. I hope you will all pass. But you must try to increase your chances. Before you go into the next room, try to move your limbs, give yourself some color. Don't walk slowly, run! Run as if you had the devil at your heels! Don't look at the SS. Run, straight in front of you!"

He paused and then added:

"And most important, don't be afraid!"

There was a piece of advice we would have loved to be able to follow.

I undressed, leaving my clothes on my cot. Tonight, there was no danger that they would be stolen.

Tibi and Yossi, who had changed Kommandos at the same time I did, came to urge me:

"Let's stay together. It will make us stronger."

Yossi was mumbling something. He probably was praying. I had never suspected that Yossi was religious. In fact, I had always believed the opposite. Tibi was silent and very pale. All the block inmates stood naked between the rows of bunks. This must be how one stands for the Last Judgment.

"They are coming!"

Three SS officers surrounded the notorious Dr. Mengele, the very same who had received us in Birkenau. The *Blockälteste* attempted a smile. He asked us:

"Ready?"

Yes, we were ready. So were the SS doctors. Dr. Mengele was holding a list: our numbers. He nodded to the *Blockälteste*: We can begin! As if this were a game.

The first to go were the "notables" of the block, the *Stubenälteste*, the Kapos, the foremen, all of whom were in perfect physical condition, of course! Then came the ordinary prisoners' turn.

Dr. Mengele looked them over from head to toe. From time to time, he noted a number. I had but one thought: not to have my number taken down and not to show my left arm.

In front of me, there were only Tibi and Yossi. They passed. I had time to notice that Mengele had not written down their numbers. Someone pushed me. It was my turn. I ran without looking back. My head was spinning: You are too skinny . . . you are too weak . . . you are too skinny, you are good for the ovens . . . The race seemed endless; I felt as though I had been running for years . . . You are too skinny, you are too weak . . . At last I arrived. Exhausted. When I had caught my breath, I asked Yossi and Tibi:

"Did they write me down?"

"No," said Yossi. Smiling, he added: "Anyway, they couldn't have. You were running too fast . . ."

I began to laugh. I was happy. I felt like kissing him. At that moment, the others did not matter! They had not written me down.

Those whose numbers had been noted were standing apart, abandoned by the whole world. Some were silently weeping.

THE SS OFFICERS LEFT. The *Blockälteste* appeared, his face reflecting our collective weariness.

"It all went well. Don't worry. Nothing will happen to anyone. Not to anyone . . ."

He was still trying to smile. A poor emaciated Jew questioned him anxiously, his voice trembling:

"But . . . sir. They *did* write me down!"

At that, the *Blockälteste* vented his anger: What! Someone refused to take his word?

"What is it now? Perhaps you think I'm lying? I'm telling you, once and for all: nothing will happen to you! Nothing! You just like to wallow in your despair, you fools!"

The bell rang, signaling that the selection had ended in the entire camp.

With all my strength I began to race toward Block 36; midway, I met my father. He came toward me:

"So? Did you pass?"

"Yes. And you?"

"Also."

We were able to breathe again. My father had a present for me: a half ration of bread, bartered for something he found at the depot, a piece of rubber that could be used to repair a shoe.

The bell. It was already time to part, to go to bed. The bell regulated everything. It gave me orders and I executed them blindly. I hated that bell. Whenever I happened to dream of a better world, I imagined a universe without a bell.

A FEW DAYS PASSED. We were no longer thinking about the selection. We went to work as usual and loaded the heavy stones onto the freight cars. The rations had grown smaller; that was the only change.

We had risen at dawn, as we did every day. We had received our black coffee, our ration of bread. We were about to head to the work yard as always. The *Blockälteste* came running:

"Let's have a moment of quiet. I have here a list of numbers. I shall read them to you. All those called will not go to work this morning; they will stay in camp."

Softly, he read some ten numbers. We understood. These were the numbers from the selection. Dr. Mengele had not forgotten.

The *Blockälteste* turned to go to his room. The ten prisoners surrounded him, clinging to his clothes:

"Save us! You promised . . . We want to go to the depot, we are strong enough to work. We are good workers. We can . . . we want . . ."

He tried to calm them, to reassure them about their fate, to explain to them that staying in the camp did not mean much, had no tragic significance: "After all, I stay here every day . . ."

The argument was more than flimsy. He realized it and, without another word, locked himself in his room.

The bell had just rung.

"Form ranks!"

Now, it no longer mattered that the work was hard. All that mattered was to be far from the block, far from the crucible of death, from the center of hell.

I saw my father running in my direction. Suddenly, I was afraid.

"What is happening?"

He was out of breath, hardly able to open his mouth.

"Me too, me too . . . They told me too to stay in the camp."

They had recorded his number without his noticing.

"What are we going to do?" I said anxiously.

But it was he who tried to reassure me:

"It's not certain yet. There's still a chance. Today, they will do another selection . . . a decisive one . . ."

I said nothing.

He felt time was running out. He was speaking rapidly, he wanted to tell me so many things. His speech became confused, his voice was choked. He knew that I had to leave in a few moments. He was going to remain alone, so alone . . .

"Here, take this knife," he said. "I won't need it anymore. You may find it useful. Also take this spoon. Don't sell it. Quickly! Go ahead, take what I'm giving you!"

My inheritance . . .

"Don't talk like that, Father." I felt on the verge of breaking into sobs. "I don't want you to say such things. Keep the spoon and knife. You will need them as much as I. We'll see each other tonight, after work."

He looked at me with his tired eyes, veiled by despair. He insisted:

"I am asking you . . . Take it, do as I ask you, my son. Time is running out. Do as your father asks you . . ."

Our Kapo shouted the order to march.

The Kommando headed toward the camp gate. Left, right! I was biting my lips. My father had remained near the block, leaning against the wall. Then he began to run, to try to catch up with us. Perhaps he had forgotten to tell me something . . . But we were marching too fast . . . Left, right!

We were at the gate. We were being counted. Around us, the din of military music. Then we were outside.

ALL DAY, I plodded around like a sleepwalker. Tibi and Yossi would call out to me, from time to time, trying to reassure me. As did the Kapo who had given me easier tasks that day. I felt sick at heart. How kindly they treated me. Like an orphan. I thought: Even now, my father is helping me.

I myself didn't know whether I wanted the day to go by quickly or not. I was afraid of finding myself alone that evening. How good it would be to die right here!

At last, we began the return journey. How I longed for an order to run! The military march. The gate. The camp. I ran toward Block 36.

Were there still miracles on this earth? He was alive. He had passed the second selection. He had still proved his usefulness . . . I gave him back his knife and spoon.

AKIBA DRUMER HAS LEFT US, a victim of the selection. Lately, he had been wandering among us, his eyes glazed, telling everyone how weak he was: "I can't go on . . . It's over . . ." We tried to raise his spirits, but he wouldn't listen to anything we said. He just kept repeating that it was all over for him, that he could no longer fight, he had no more strength, no more faith. His eyes would suddenly go blank, leaving two gaping wounds, two wells of terror.

He was not alone in having lost his faith during those days of selection. I knew a rabbi, from a small town in Poland. He was old and bent, his lips constantly trembling. He was always praying, in the block, at work, in the ranks. He recited entire pages from the Talmud, arguing with himself, asking and answering himself endless questions. One day, he said to me:

"It's over. God is no longer with us."

And as though he regretted having uttered such words so coldly, so dryly, he added in his broken voice: "I know. No one has the right to say things like that. I know that very well. Man is too insignificant, too limited, to even try to comprehend God's mysterious ways. But what can someone like myself do? I'm neither a sage nor a just man. I am not a saint. I'm a simple creature of flesh and bone. I suffer hell in my soul and my flesh. I also have eyes and I see what is being done here. Where is God's mercy? Where's God? How can I believe, how can anyone believe in this God of Mercy?"

Poor Akiba Drumer, if only he could have kept his faith in God, if only he could have considered this suffering a divine test, he would not have been swept away by the selection. But as soon as he felt the first chinks in his faith, he lost all incentive to fight and opened the door to death.

When the selection came, he was doomed from the start,

offering his neck to the executioner, as it were. All he asked of us was:

"In three days, I'll be gone . . . Say Kaddish for me."

We promised: in three days, when we would see the smoke rising from the chimney, we would think of him. We would gather ten men and hold a special service. All his friends would say Kaddish.

Then he left, in the direction of the hospital. His step was almost steady and he never looked back. An ambulance was waiting to take him to Birkenau.

There followed terrible days. We received more blows than food. The work was crushing. And three days after he left, we forgot to say Kaddish.

WINTER HAD ARRIVED. The days became short and the nights almost unbearable. From the first hours of dawn, a glacial wind lashed us like a whip. We were handed winter clothing: striped shirts that were a bit heavier. The veterans grabbed the opportunity for further sniggering:

"Now you'll really get a taste of camp!"

We went off to work as usual, our bodies frozen. The stones were so cold that, touching them, we felt that our hands would remain stuck. But we got used to that too.

Christmas and New Year's we did not work. We were treated to a slightly less transparent soup.

Around the middle of January, my right foot began to swell from the cold. I could not stand on it. I went to the infirmary. The doctor, a great Jewish doctor, a prisoner like ourselves, was categorical: "We have to operate! If we wait, the toes and perhaps the leg will have to be amputated."

That was all I needed! But I had no choice. The doctor had

decided to operate and there could be no discussion. In fact, I was rather glad that the decision had been his.

They put me in a bed with white sheets. I had forgotten that people slept in sheets.

Actually, being in the infirmary was not bad at all: we were entitled to good bread, a thicker soup. No more bell, no more roll call, no more work. From time to time, I was able to send a piece of bread to my father.

Next to me lay a Hungarian Jew suffering from dysentery. He was skin and bones, his eyes were dead. I could just hear his voice, the only indication that he was alive. Where did he get the strength to speak?

"Don't rejoice too soon, son. Here too there is selection. In fact, more often than outside. Germany has no need of sick Jews. Germany has no need of me. When the next transport arrives, you'll have a new neighbor. Therefore, listen to me: leave the infirmary before the next selection!"

These words, coming from the grave, as it were, from a faceless shape, filled me with terror. True, the infirmary was very small, and if new patients were to arrive, room would have to be made.

But then perhaps my faceless neighbor, afraid of being among the first displaced, simply wanted to get rid of me, to free my bed, to give himself a chance to survive . . . Perhaps he only wanted to frighten me. But then again, what if he was telling the truth? I decided to wait and see.

THE DOCTOR came to tell me that he would operate the next day.

"Don't be afraid," he said. "Everything will be all right."

At ten o'clock in the morning, I was taken to the operating room. My doctor was there. That reassured me. I felt that, in his presence, nothing serious could happen to me. Every one of his words was healing and every glance of his carried a message of hope. "It will hurt a little," he said, "but it will pass. Be brave."

The operation lasted one hour. They did not put me to sleep. I did not take my eyes off my doctor. Then I felt myself sink . . .

When I came to and opened my eyes, I first saw nothing but a huge expanse of white, my sheets, then I saw my doctor's face above me:

"Everything went well. You have spunk, my boy. Next, you'll stay here two weeks for some proper rest and that will be it. You'll eat well, you'll relax your body and your nerves . . ."

All I could do was follow the movements of his lips. I barely understood what he was telling me, but the inflection of his voice soothed me. Suddenly, I broke into a cold sweat; I couldn't feel my leg! Had they amputated it?

"Doctor," I stammered. "Doctor?"

"What is it, son?"

I didn't have the courage to ask him.

"Doctor, I'm thirsty . . ."

He had water brought to me . . . He was smiling. He was ready to walk out, to see other patients.

"Doctor?"

"Yes?"

"Will I be able to use my leg?"

He stopped smiling. I became very frightened. He said, "Listen, son. Do you trust me?"

"Very much, Doctor."

"Then listen well: in two weeks you'll be fully recovered. You'll be able to walk like the others. The sole of your foot was full of pus. I just had to open the sac. Your leg was not amputated. You'll see, in two weeks, you'll be walking around like everybody else."

All I had to do was wait two weeks.

BUT TWO DAYS AFTER my operation, rumors swept through the camp that the battlefront had suddenly drawn nearer. The Red Army was racing toward Buna: it was only a matter of hours.

We were quite used to this kind of rumor. It wasn't the first time that false prophets announced to us: peace-in-the-world, the-Red-Cross-negotiating-our-liberation, or other fables . . . And often we would believe them . . . It was like an injection of morphine.

Only this time, these prophecies seemed more founded. During the last nights we had heard the cannons in the distance.

My faceless neighbor spoke up:

"Don't be deluded. Hitler has made it clear that he will annihilate all Jews before the clock strikes twelve."

I exploded:

"What do you care what he said? Would you want us to consider him a prophet?"

His cold eyes stared at me. At last, he said wearily:

"I have more faith in Hitler than in anyone else. He alone has kept his promises, all his promises, to the Jewish people."

THAT AFTERNOON AT FOUR O'CLOCK, as usual, the bell called all the *Blockälteste* for their daily report.

They came back shattered. They had difficulty opening their mouths. All they could utter was one word: "Evacuation." The camp was going to be emptied and we would be sent to the rear. Where to? Somewhere in deepest Germany. To other camps; there was no shortage of them.

"When?"

"Tomorrow night."

"Perhaps the Russians will arrive before . . ."

"Perhaps."

We knew perfectly well they would not.

The camp had become a hive of activity. People were running, calling to one another. In every block, the inmates prepared for the journey ahead. I had forgotten about my lame foot. A doctor came into the room and announced:

"Tomorrow, right after nightfall, the camp will start on its march. Block by block. The sick can remain in the infirmary. They will not be evacuated."

That news made us wonder. Were the SS really going to leave hundreds of prisoners behind in the infirmaries, pending the arrival of their liberators? Were they really going to allow Jews to hear the clock strike twelve? Of course not.

"All the patients will be finished off on the spot," said the faceless one. "And in one last swoop, thrown into the furnaces."

"Surely, the camp will be mined," said another. "Right after the evacuation, it will all blow up."

As for me, I was thinking not about death but about not wanting to be separated from my father. We had already suffered so much, endured so much together. This was not the moment to separate.

I ran outside to look for him. The snow was piled high; the blocks' windows veiled in frost. Holding a shoe in my hand, for I could not put it on my right foot, I ran, feeling neither pain nor cold.

"What are we going to do?"

My father didn't answer.

"What are we going to do?"

He was lost in thought. The choice was in our hands. For once. We could decide our fate for ourselves. To stay, both of us, in the infirmary, where, thanks to my doctor, he could enter as either a patient or a medic.

I had made up my mind to accompany my father wherever he went.

"Well, Father, what do we do?"

He was silent.

"Let's be evacuated with the others," I said.

He didn't answer. He was looking at my foot.

"You think you'll be able to walk?"

"Yes, I think so."

"Let's hope we won't regret it, Eliezer."

AFTER THE WAR, I learned the fate of those who had remained at the infirmary. They were, quite simply, liberated by the Russians, two days after the evacuation.

I DID NOT RETURN to the infirmary. I went straight to my block. My wound had reopened and was bleeding: the snow under my feet turned red.

The *Blockälteste* distributed double rations of bread and margarine for the road. We could take as much clothing from the store as we wanted.

It was cold. We got into our bunks. The last night in Buna. Once more, the last night. The last night at home, the last night in the ghetto, the last night in the cattle car, and, now, the last night in Buna. How much longer would our lives be lived from one "last night" to the next?

I didn't sleep. Through the frosty windowpanes we could see flashes of red. Cannon shots broke the silence of night. How close the Russians were! Between them and us—one night—our last. There was whispering from one bunk to the other; with a little luck, the Russians would be here before the evacuation. Hope was still alive.

Someone called out:

"Try to sleep. Gather your strength for the journey."

It reminded me of my mother's last recommendations in the ghetto. But I couldn't fall asleep. My foot was on fire.

IN THE MORNING, the camp did not look the same. The prisoners showed up in all kinds of strange garb; it looked like a masquerade. We each had put on several garments, one over the other, to better protect ourselves from the cold. Poor clowns, wider than tall, more dead than alive, poor creatures whose ghostly faces peeked out from layers of prisoner's clothes! Poor clowns!

I tried to find a very large shoe. In vain. I tore my blanket and wrapped it around my foot. Then I went off to wander through the camp in search of a little more bread and a few potatoes. Some people said we would be going to Czechoslovakia. No: to Gros-Rosen. No: to Gleiwitz. No: to . . .

TWO O'CLOCK in the afternoon. The snow continued to fall heavily.

Now the hours were passing quickly. Dusk had fallen. Daylight disappeared into a gray mist.

Suddenly the *Blockälteste* remembered that we had forgotten to clean the block. He commanded four prisoners to mop the floor . . . One hour before leaving camp! Why? For whom?

"For the liberating army," he told us. "Let them know that here lived men and not pigs."

So we were men after all? The block was cleaned from top to bottom.

AT SIX O'CLOCK the bell rang. The death knell. The funeral. The procession was beginning its march.

"Fall in! Quickly!"

In a few moments, we stood in ranks. Block by block. Night had fallen. Everything was happening according to plan.

The searchlights came on. Hundreds of SS appeared out of the darkness, accompanied by police dogs. The snow continued to fall.

The gates of the camp opened. It seemed as though an even darker night was waiting for us on the other side.

The first blocks began to march. We waited. We had to await the exodus of the fifty-six blocks that preceded us. It was very cold. In my pocket, I had two pieces of bread. How I would have liked to eat them! But I knew I must not. Not yet.

Our turn was coming: Block 53 . . . Block 55 . . .

"Block 57, forward! March!"

It snowed on and on.

A N ICY WIND WAS BLOWING VIOLENTLY. But we marched without faltering.

The SS made us increase our pace. "Faster, you tramps, you flea-ridden dogs!" Why not? Moving fast made us a little warmer. The blood flowed more readily in our veins. We had the feeling of being alive . . .

"Faster, you filthy dogs!" We were no longer marching, we were running. Like automatons. The SS were running as well, weapons in hand. We looked as though we were running from them.

The night was pitch-black. From time to time, a shot exploded in the darkness. They had orders to shoot anyone who could not sustain the pace. Their fingers on the triggers, they did not deprive themselves of the pleasure. If one of us stopped for a second, a quick shot eliminated the filthy dog.

I was putting one foot in front of the other, like a machine. I was dragging this emaciated body that was still such a weight. If only I could have shed it! Though I tried to put it out of my mind, I couldn't help thinking that there were two of us: my body and I. And I hated that body. I kept repeating to myself:

"Don't think, don't stop, run!"

Near me, men were collapsing into the dirty snow. Gunshots.

A young boy from Poland was marching beside me. His name was Zalman. He had worked in the electrical material depot in Buna. People mocked him because he was forever praying or meditating on some Talmudic question. For him, it was an escape from reality, from feeling the blows . . .

All of a sudden, he had terrible stomach cramps.

"My stomach aches," he whispered to me. He couldn't go on. He had to stop a moment. I begged him: "Wait a little, Zalman. Soon, we will all come to a halt. We cannot run like this to the end of the world."

But, while running, he began to undo his buttons and yelled to me:

"I can't go on. My stomach is bursting . . ."

"Make an effort, Zalman . . . Try . . ."

"I can't go on," he groaned.

He lowered his pants and fell to the ground.

That is the image I have of him.

I don't believe that he was finished off by an SS, for nobody had noticed. He must have died, trampled under the feet of the thousands of men who followed us.

I soon forgot him. I began to think of myself again. Because of my numb foot, I shivered with every step. Just a few more meters and it will be over. I'll fall. A small red flame . . . A shot . . . Death enveloped me, it suffocated me. It stuck to me like glue. I felt I could touch it. The idea of dying, of ceasing to be, began to fascinate me. To no longer exist. To no longer feel the excruciating pain of my foot. To no longer feel anything, neither fatigue, nor cold, nothing. To break rank, to let myself slide to the side of the road . . .

My father's presence was the only thing that stopped me. He was running next to me, out of breath, out of strength, desperate.

I had no right to let myself die. What would he do without me? I was his sole support.

These thoughts were going through my mind as I continued to run, not feeling my numb foot, not even realizing that I was still running, that I still owned a body that galloped down the road among thousands of others.

When I became conscious of myself again, I tried to slow my pace somewhat. But there was no way. These human waves were rolling forward and would have crushed me like an ant.

By now, I moved like a sleepwalker. I sometimes closed my eyes and it was like running while asleep. Now and then, someone kicked me violently from behind and I would wake up. The man in back of me was screaming, "Run faster. If you don't want to move, let us pass you." But all I had to do was close my eyes to see a whole world pass before me, to dream of another life.

The road was endless. To allow oneself to be carried by the mob, to be swept away by blind fate. When the SS were tired, they were replaced. But no one replaced us. Chilled to the bone, our throats parched, famished, out of breath, we pressed on.

We were the masters of nature, the masters of the world. We had transcended everything—death, fatigue, our natural needs. We were stronger than cold and hunger, stronger than the guns and the desire to die, doomed and rootless, nothing but numbers, we were the only men on earth.

At last, the morning star appeared in the gray sky. A hesitant light began to hover on the horizon. We were exhausted, we had lost all strength, all illusion.

The Kommandant announced that we had already covered twenty kilometers since we left. Long since, we had exceeded the limits of fatigue. Our legs moved mechanically, in spite of us, without us.

We came to an abandoned village. Not a living soul. Not a single bark. Houses with gaping windows. A few people slipped out of the ranks, hoping to hide in some abandoned building.

One more hour of marching and, at last, the order to halt.

As one man, we let ourselves sink into the snow. My father shook me:

"Not here . . . Get up . . . A little farther down. There is a shed over there . . . Come . . ."

I had neither the desire nor the resolve to get up. Yet I obeyed. It was not really a shed, but a brick factory whose roof had fallen in. Its windowpanes were shattered, its walls covered in soot. It was not easy to get inside. Hundreds of prisoners jostled one another at the door.

We finally succeeded in entering. Inside, too, the snow was thick. I let myself slide to the ground. Only now did I feel the full extent of my weakness. The snow seemed to me like a very soft, very warm carpet. I fell asleep. I don't know how long I slept. A few minutes or one hour. When I woke up, a frigid hand was tapping my cheeks. I tried to open my eyes: it was my father.

How he had aged since last night! His body was completely twisted, shriveled up into himself. His eyes were glazed over, his lips parched, decayed. Everything about him expressed total exhaustion. His voice was damp from tears and snow.

"Don't let yourself be overcome by sleep, Eliezer. It's dangerous to fall asleep in snow. One falls asleep forever. Come, my son, come . . . Get up."

Get up? How could I? How was I to leave this warm blanket? I was hearing my father's words, but their meaning escaped me, as if he had asked me to carry the entire shed in my arms . . .

"Come, my son, come . . ."

I got up, with clenched teeth. Holding on to me with one arm, he led me outside. It was not easy. It was as difficult to go out as to come in. Beneath our feet there lay men, crushed, trampled underfoot, dying. Nobody paid attention to them.

We were outside. The icy wind whipped my face. I was constantly biting my lips so that they wouldn't freeze. All around me, what appeared to be a dance of death. My head was reeling. I was walking through a cemetery. Among the stiffened corpses, there were logs of wood. Not a sound of distress, not a plaintive cry, nothing but mass agony and silence. Nobody asked anyone for help. One died because one had to. No point in making trouble.

I saw myself in every stiffened corpse. Soon I wouldn't even be seeing them anymore; I would be one of them. A matter of hours.

"Come Father, let's go back to the shed . . ."

He didn't answer. He was not even looking at the dead.

"Come, Father. It's better there. You'll be able to lie down. We'll take turns. I'll watch over you and you'll watch over me. We won't let each other fall asleep. We'll look after each other."

He accepted. After trampling over many bodies and corpses, we succeeded in getting inside. We let ourselves fall to the ground.

"Don't worry, son. Go to sleep. I'll watch over you."

"You first, Father. Sleep."

He refused. I stretched out and tried to sleep, to doze a little, but in vain. God knows what I would have given to be able to sleep a few moments. But deep inside, I knew that to sleep meant to die. And something in me rebelled against that death. Death, which was settling in all around me, silently, gently. It would seize upon a sleeping person, steal into him and devour him bit by bit. Next to me, someone was trying to awaken his neighbor, his brother, perhaps, or his comrade. In vain. Defeated, he lay down too, next to the corpse, and also fell asleep. Who would wake him up? Reaching out with my arm, I touched him:

"Wake up. One mustn't fall asleep here . . ."

He half opened his eyes.

"No advice," he said, his voice a whisper. "I'm exhausted. Mind your business, leave me alone."

My father too was gently dozing. I couldn't see his eyes. His cap was covering his face.

"Wake up," I whispered in his ear.

He awoke with a start. He sat up, bewildered, stunned, like an orphan. He looked all around him, taking it all in as if he had suddenly decided to make an inventory of his universe, to determine where he was and how and why he was there. Then he smiled.

I shall always remember that smile. What world did it come from?

Heavy snow continued to fall over the corpses.

The door of the shed opened. An old man appeared. His mustache was covered with ice, his lips were blue. It was Rabbi Eliahu, who had headed a small congregation in Poland. A very kind man, beloved by everyone in the camp, even by the Kapos and the *Blockälteste*. Despite the ordeals and deprivations, his face continued to radiate his innocence. He was the only rabbi whom nobody ever failed to address as "Rabbi" in Buna. He looked like one of those prophets of old, always in the midst of his people when they needed to be consoled. And, strangely, his words never provoked anyone. They did bring peace.

As he entered the shed, his eyes, brighter than ever, seemed to be searching for someone:

"Perhaps someone here has seen my son?"

He had lost his son in the commotion. He had searched for him among the dying, to no avail. Then he had dug through the snow to find his body. In vain.

For three years, they had stayed close to one another. Side by side, they had endured the suffering, the blows; they had waited for their ration of bread and they had prayed. Three years, from camp to camp, from selection to selection. And now—when the end seemed near—fate had separated them.

When he came near me, Rabbi Eliahu whispered, "It happened on the road. We lost sight of one another during the journey. I fell behind a little, at the rear of the column. I didn't have the strength to run anymore. And my son didn't notice. That's all I know. Where has he disappeared? Where can I find him? Perhaps you've seen him somewhere?"

"No, Rabbi Eliahu, I haven't seen him."

And so he left, as he had come: a shadow swept away by the wind.

He had already gone through the door when I remembered that I had noticed his son running beside me. I had forgotten and so had not mentioned it to Rabbi Eliahu!

But then I remembered something else: his son *had* seen him losing ground, sliding back to the rear of the column. He had seen him. And he had continued to run in front, letting the distance between them become greater.

A terrible thought crossed my mind: What if he had wanted to be rid of his father? He had felt his father growing weaker and, believing that the end was near, had thought by this separation to free himself of a burden that could diminish his own chance for survival.

It was good that I *had* forgotten all that. And I was glad that Rabbi Eliahu continued to search for his beloved son.

And in spite of myself, a prayer formed inside me, a prayer to this God in whom I no longer believed.

"Oh God, Master of the Universe, give me the strength never to do what Rabbi Eliahu's son has done."

There was shouting outside, in the courtyard. Night had fallen and the SS were ordering us to form ranks.

We started to march once more. The dead remained in the yard, under the snow without even a marker, like fallen guards. No one recited Kaddish over them. Sons abandoned the remains of their fathers without a tear.

On the road, it snowed and snowed, it snowed endlessly. We were marching more slowly. Even the guards seemed tired. My wounded foot no longer hurt, probably frozen. I felt I had lost that foot. It had become detached from me like a wheel fallen off a car. Never mind. I had to accept the fact: I would have to live with only one leg. The important thing was not to dwell on it. Especially now. Leave those thoughts for later.

Our column had lost all appearance of discipline. Everyone walked as he wished, as he could. No more gunshots. Our guards surely *were* tired.

But death hardly needed their help. The cold was conscientiously doing its work. At every step, somebody fell down and ceased to suffer.

From time to time, SS officers on motorcycles drove the length of the column to shake off the growing apathy:

"Hold on! We're almost there!"

"Courage! Just a few more hours!"

"We're arriving in Gleiwitz!"

These words of encouragement, even coming as they did from the mouths of our assassins, were of great help. Nobody wanted to give up now, just before the end, so close to our destination. Our eyes searched the horizon for the barbed wire of Gleiwitz. Our only wish was to arrive there quickly.

By now it was night. It had stopped snowing. We marched a few more hours before we arrived. We saw the camp only when we stood right in front of its gate.

The Kapos quickly settled us into the barrack. There was shoving and jostling as if this were the ultimate haven, the gateway to life. People trod over numbed bodies, trampled wounded faces. There were no cries, only a few moans. My father and I were thrown to the ground by this rolling tide. From beneath me came a desperate cry:

"You're crushing me . . . Have mercy!"

The voice was familiar.

"You're crushing me . . . Mercy, have mercy!"

The same faint voice, the same cry I had heard somewhere before. This voice had spoken to me one day. When? Years ago? No, it must have been in the camp.

"Mercy!"

I felt that I was crushing him, preventing him from breathing, I wanted to get up and disengage myself to allow him to breathe. But I myself was crushed under the weight of other bodies. I had difficulty breathing. I dug my nails into unknown faces. I was biting my way through, searching for air. No one cried out.

Suddenly I remembered. Juliek! The boy from Warsaw who played the violin in the Buna orchestra . . .

"Juliek, is that you?"

"Eliezer . . . The twenty-five whiplashes . . . Yes . . . I remember."

He fell silent. A long moment went by.

"Juliek! Can you hear me, Juliek?"

"Yes . . ." he said feebly. "What do you want?"

He was not dead.

"Are you all right, Juliek?" I asked, less to know his answer than to hear him speak, to know he was alive.

"All right, Eliezer . . . All right . . . Not too much air . . . Tired. My feet are swollen. It's good to rest, but my violin . . ."

I thought he'd lost his mind. His violin? Here?

"What about your violin?"

He was gasping:

"I . . . I'm afraid . . . They'll break . . . my violin . . . I . . . I brought it with me."

I could not answer him. Someone had lain down on top of me, smothering me. I couldn't breathe through my mouth or my nose. Sweat was running down my forehead and my back. This was it; the end of the road. A silent death, suffocation. No way to scream, to call for help.

I tried to rid myself of my invisible assassin. My whole desire to live became concentrated in my nails. I scratched, I fought for a breath of air. I tore at decaying flesh that did not respond. I could not free myself of that mass weighing down my chest. Who knows? Was I struggling with a dead man?

I shall never know. All I can say is that I prevailed. I succeeded in digging a hole in that wall of dead and dying people, a small hole through which I could drink a little air.

"FATHER, ARE YOU THERE?" I asked as soon as I was able to utter a word.

I knew that he could not be far from me.

"Yes!" a voice replied from far away, as if from another world. "I am trying to sleep."

He was trying to sleep. Could one fall asleep here? Wasn't it dangerous to lower one's guard, even for a moment, when death could strike at any time?

Those were my thoughts when I heard the sound of a violin. A violin in a dark barrack where the dead were piled on top of the living? Who was this madman who played the violin here, at the edge of his own grave? Or was it a hallucination?

It had to be Juliek.

He was playing a fragment of a Beethoven concerto. Never before had I heard such a beautiful sound. In such silence.

How had he succeeded in disengaging himself? To slip out from under my body without my feeling it?

The darkness enveloped us. All I could hear was the violin, and it was as if Juliek's soul had become his bow. He was playing his life. His whole being was gliding over the strings. His unfulfilled hopes. His charred past, his extinguished future. He played that which he would never play again.

I shall never forget Juliek. How could I forget this concert given before an audience of the dead and dying? Even today, when I hear that particular piece by Beethoven, my eyes close and out of the darkness emerges the pale and melancholy face of my Polish comrade bidding farewell to an audience of dying men.

I don't know how long he played. I was overcome by sleep. When I awoke at daybreak, I saw Juliek facing me, hunched over, dead. Next to him lay his violin, trampled, an eerily poignant little corpse.

WE STAYED IN GLEIWITZ for three days. Days without food or water. We were forbidden to leave the barrack. The door was guarded by the SS.

I was hungry and thirsty. I must have been very dirty and disheveled, to judge by what the others looked like. The bread we had brought from Buna had been devoured long since. And who knew when we would be given another ration?

The front followed us. We could again hear the cannons very close by. But we no longer had the strength or the courage to think that the Germans would run out of time, that the Russians would reach us before we could be evacuated.

We learned that we would be moved to the center of Germany.

On the third day, at dawn, we were driven out of the barrack. We threw blankets over our shoulders, like prayer shawls. We were directed to a gate that divided the camp in two. A group of SS officers stood waiting. A word flew through our ranks: selection!

The SS officers were doing the selection: the weak to the left; those who walked well, to the right.

My father was sent to the left. I ran after him. An SS officer shouted at my back:

"Come back!"

I inched my way through the crowd. Several SS men rushed to find me, creating such confusion that a number of people were able to switch over to the right—among them my father and I. Still, there were gunshots and some dead.

We were led out of the camp. After a half-hour march, we arrived in the very middle of a field crossed by railroad tracks. This was where we were to wait for the train's arrival.

Snow was falling heavily. We were forbidden to sit down or to move.

A thick layer of snow was accumulating on our blankets. We were given bread, the usual ration. We threw ourselves on it. Someone had the idea of quenching his thirst by eating snow. Soon, we were all imitating him. As we were not permitted to bend down, we took out our spoons and ate the snow off our neighbor's backs. A mouthful of bread and a spoonful of snow. The SS men who were watching were greatly amused by the spectacle.

The hours went by. Our eyes were tired from staring at the horizon, waiting for the liberating train to appear. It arrived only very late that evening. An infinitely long train, composed of roofless cattle cars. The SS shoved us inside, a hundred per car: we were so skinny! When everybody was on board, the convoy left.

P RESSED TIGHTLY AGAINST ONE ANOTHER, in an effort to resist the cold, our heads empty and heavy, our brains a whirlwind of decaying memories. Our minds numb with indifference. Here or elsewhere, what did it matter? Die today or tomorrow, or later? The night was growing longer, never-ending.

When at last a grayish light appeared on the horizon, it revealed a tangle of human shapes, heads sunk deeply between the shoulders, crouching, piled one on top of the other, like a cemetery covered with snow. In the early dawn light, I tried to distinguish between the living and those who were no more. But there was barely a difference. My gaze remained fixed on someone who, eyes wide open, stared into space. His colorless face was covered with a layer of frost and snow.

My father had huddled near me, draped in his blanket, shoulders laden with snow. And what if he were dead, as well? I called out to him. No response. I would have screamed if I could have. He was not moving.

Suddenly, the evidence overwhelmed me: there was no longer any reason to live, any reason to fight.

The train stopped in an empty field. The abrupt halt had wakened a few sleepers. They stood, looking around, startled.

Outside, the SS walked by, shouting:

"Throw out all the dead! Outside, all the corpses!"

The living were glad. They would have more room. Volunteers began the task. They touched those who had remained on the ground.

"Here's one! Take him!"

The volunteers undressed him and eagerly shared his garments. Then, two "gravediggers" grabbed him by the head and feet and threw him from the wagon, like a sack of flour.

There was shouting all around:

"Come on! Here's another! My neighbor. He's not moving . . ."

I woke from my apathy only when two men approached my father. I threw myself on his body. He was cold. I slapped him. I rubbed his hands, crying:

"Father! Father! Wake up. They're going to throw you outside . . ."

His body remained inert.

The two "gravediggers" had grabbed me by the neck:

"Leave him alone. Can't you see that he's dead?"

"No!" I yelled. "He's not dead! Not yet!"

And I started to hit him harder and harder. At last, my father half opened his eyes. They were glassy. He was breathing faintly.

"You see," I cried.

The two men went away.

Twenty corpses were thrown from our wagon. Then the train resumed its journey, leaving in its wake, in a snowy field in Poland, hundreds of naked orphans without a tomb.

———

WE RECEIVED NO FOOD. We lived on snow; it took the place of bread. The days resembled the nights, and the nights left in our souls the dregs of their darkness. The train rolled slowly, often halted for a few hours, and continued. It never stopped snowing. We remained lying on the floor for days and nights, one on top of the other, never uttering a word. We were nothing but frozen bodies. Our eyes closed, we merely waited for the next stop, to unload our dead.

THERE FOLLOWED days and nights of traveling. Occasionally, we would pass through German towns. Usually, very early in the morning. German laborers were going to work. They would stop and look at us without surprise.

One day when we had come to a stop, a worker took a piece of bread out of his bag and threw it into a wagon. There was a stampede. Dozens of starving men fought desperately over a few crumbs. The worker watched the spectacle with great interest.

YEARS LATER, I witnessed a similar spectacle in Aden. Our ship's passengers amused themselves by throwing coins to the "natives," who dove to retrieve them. An elegant Parisian lady took great pleasure in this game. When I noticed two children desperately fighting in the water, one trying to strangle the other, I implored the lady:

"Please, don't throw any more coins!"

"Why not?" said she. "I like to give charity . . ."

IN THE WAGON where the bread had landed, a battle had ensued. Men were hurling themselves against each other, trampling, tearing at and mauling each other. Beasts of prey unleashed, animal hate in their eyes. An extraordinary vitality possessed them, sharpening their teeth and nails.

A crowd of workmen and curious passersby had formed all along the train. They had undoubtedly never seen a train with this kind of cargo. Soon, pieces of bread were falling into the wagons from all sides. And the spectators observed these emaciated creatures ready to kill for a crust of bread.

A piece fell into our wagon. I decided not to move. Anyway, I knew that I would not be strong enough to fight off dozens of violent men! I saw, not far from me, an old man dragging himself on all fours. He had just detached himself from the struggling mob. He was holding one hand to his heart. At first I thought he had received a blow to his chest. Then I understood: he was hiding a piece of bread under his shirt. With lightning speed he pulled it out and put it to his mouth. His eyes lit up, a smile, like a grimace, illuminated his ashen face. And was immediately extinguished. A shadow had lain down beside him. And this shadow threw itself over him. Stunned by the blows, the old man was crying:

"Meir, my little Meir! Don't you recognize me . . . You're killing your father . . . I have bread . . . for you too . . . for you too . . ."

He collapsed. But his fist was still clutching a small crust. He wanted to raise it to his mouth. But the other threw himself on him. The old man mumbled something, groaned, and died. Nobody cared. His son searched him, took the crust of bread, and began to devour it. He didn't get far. Two men had been watching him. They jumped him. Others joined in. When they withdrew, there were two dead bodies next to me, the father and the son.

I was sixteen.

IN OUR WAGON, there was a friend of my father's, Meir Katz. He had worked as a gardener in Buna and from time to time had brought us some green vegetables. Less undernourished than the rest of us, detention had been easier on him. Because he was stronger than most of us, he had been put in charge of our wagon.

On the third night of our journey, I woke up with a start when I felt two hands on my throat, trying to strangle me. I barely had time to call out:

"Father!"

Just that one word. I was suffocating. But my father had awakened and grabbed my aggressor. Too weak to overwhelm him, he thought of calling Meir Katz:

"Come, come quickly! Someone is strangling my son!"

In a few moments, I was freed. I never did find out why this stranger had wanted to strangle me.

But days later, Meir Katz told my father:

"Shlomo, I am getting weak. My strength is gone. I won't make it . . ."

"Don't give in!" my father tried to encourage him. "You must resist! Don't lose faith in yourself!"

But Meir Katz only groaned in response:

"I can't go on, Shlomo! . . . I can't help it . . . I can't go on . . ."

My father took his arm. And Meir Katz, the strong one, the sturdiest of us all, began to cry. His son had been taken from him during the first selection but only now was he crying for him. Only now did he fall apart. He could not go on. He had reached the end.

On the last day of our journey, a terrible wind began to blow. And the snow kept falling. We sensed that the end was near; the real end. We could not hold out long in this glacial wind, this storm.

Somebody got up and yelled:

"We must not remain sitting. We shall freeze to death! Let's get up and move . . ."

We all got up. We all pulled our soaked blankets tighter around our shoulders. And we tried to take a few steps, to shuffle back and forth, in place.

Suddenly, a cry rose in the wagon, the cry of a wounded animal. Someone had just died.

Others, close to death, imitated his cry. And their cries seemed to come from beyond the grave. Soon everybody was crying. Groaning. Moaning. Cries of distress hurled into the wind and the snow.

The lament spread from wagon to wagon. It was contagious. And now hundreds of cries rose at once. The death rattle of an entire convoy with the end approaching. All boundaries had been crossed. Nobody had any strength left. And the night seemed endless.

Meir Katz was moaning:

"Why don't they just shoot us now?"

That same night, we reached our destination.

It was late. The guards came to unload us. The dead were left in the wagons. Only those who could stand could leave.

Meir Katz remained on the train. The last day had been the most lethal. We had been a hundred or so in this wagon. Twelve of us left it. Among them, my father and myself.

We had arrived in Buchenwald.

A T THE ENTRANCE to the camp, SS officers were waiting for us. We were counted. Then we were directed to the *Appelplatz*. The orders were given over the loudspeakers:

"Form ranks of five! Groups of one hundred! Five steps forward!"

I tightened my grip on my father's hand. The old, familiar fear: not to lose him.

Very close to us stood the tall chimney of the crematorium's furnace. It no longer impressed us. It barely drew our attention.

A veteran of Buchenwald told us that we would be taking a shower and afterward be sent to different blocks. The idea of a hot shower fascinated me. My father didn't say a word. He was breathing heavily beside me.

"Father," I said, "just another moment. Soon, we'll be able to lie down. You'll be able to rest . . ."

He didn't answer. I myself was so weary that his silence left me indifferent. My only wish was to take the shower as soon as possible and lie down on a cot.

Only it wasn't easy to reach the showers. Hundreds of prisoners crowded the area. The guards seemed unable to restore order. They were lashing out, left and right, to no avail. Some prisoners who didn't have the strength to jostle, or even to stand, sat down in the snow. My father wanted to do the same. He was moaning:

"I can't anymore . . . It's over . . . I shall die right here . . ."

He dragged me toward a pile of snow from which protruded human shapes, torn blankets.

"Leave me," he said. "I can't go on anymore . . . Have pity on me . . . I'll wait here until we can go into the showers . . . You'll come and get me."

I could have screamed in anger. To have lived and endured so much; was I going to let my father die now? Now that we would be able to take a good hot shower and lie down?

"Father!" I howled. "Father! Get up! Right now! You will kill yourself . . ."

And I grabbed his arm. He continued to moan:

"Don't yell, my son . . . Have pity on your old father . . . Let me rest here . . . A little . . . I beg of you, I'm so tired . . . no more strength . . ."

He had become childlike: weak, frightened, vulnerable.

"Father," I said, "you cannot stay here."

I pointed to the corpses around him; they too had wanted to rest here.

"I see, my son. I do see them. Let them sleep. They haven't closed an eye for so long . . . They're exhausted . . . exhausted . . ."

His voice was tender.

I howled into the wind:

"They're dead! They will never wake up! Never! Do you understand?"

This discussion continued for some time. I knew that I was no longer arguing with him but with Death itself, with Death that he had already chosen.

The sirens began to wail. Alert. The lights went out in the entire camp. The guards chased us toward the blocks. In a flash, there was no one left outside. We were only too glad not to have to stay outside any longer, in the freezing wind. We let ourselves sink into the floor. The cauldrons at the entrance found no takers. There were several tiers of bunks. To sleep was all that mattered.

WHEN I WOKE UP, it was daylight. That is when I remembered that I had a father. During the alert, I had followed the mob, not taking care of him. I knew he was running out of strength, close to death, and yet I had abandoned him.

I went to look for him.

Yet at the same time a thought crept into my mind: If only I didn't find him! If only I were relieved of this responsibility, I could use all my strength to fight for my own survival, to take care only of myself . . . Instantly, I felt ashamed, ashamed of myself forever.

I walked for hours without finding him. Then I came to a block where they were distributing black "coffee." People stood in line, quarreled.

A plaintive voice came from behind me:

"Eliezer, my son. . . . bring me . . . a little coffee . . ."

I ran toward him.

"Father! I've been looking for you for so long . . . Where were you? Did you sleep? How are you feeling?"

He seemed to be burning with fever. I fought my way to the coffee cauldron like a wild beast. And I succeeded in bringing back a cup. I took one gulp. The rest was for him.

I shall never forget the gratitude that shone in his eyes when he swallowed this beverage. The gratitude of a wounded animal. With these few mouthfuls of hot water, I had probably given him more satisfaction than during my entire childhood . . .

He was lying on the boards, ashen, his lips pale and dry, shivering. I couldn't stay with him any longer. We had been ordered to go outside to allow for cleaning of the blocks. Only the sick could remain inside.

We stayed outside for five hours. We were given soup. When they allowed us to return to the blocks, I rushed toward my father:

"Did you eat?"

"No."

"Why?"

"They didn't give us anything . . . They said that we were sick, that we would die soon, and that it would be a waste of food . . . I can't go on . . ."

I gave him what was left of my soup. But my heart was heavy. I was aware that I was doing it grudgingly.

Just like Rabbi Eliahu's son, I had not passed the test.

EVERY DAY, my father was getting weaker. His eyes were watery, his face the color of dead leaves. On the third day after we arrived in Buchenwald, everybody had to go to the showers. Even the sick, who were instructed to go last.

When we returned from the showers, we had to wait outside a long time. The cleaning of the blocks had not been completed.

From afar, I saw my father and ran to meet him. He went by me like a shadow, passing me without stopping, without a glance. I called to him, he did not turn around. I ran after him:

"Father, where are you running?"

He looked at me for a moment and his gaze was distant, otherworldly, the face of a stranger. It lasted only a moment and then he ran away.

SUFFERING FROM A BOUT OF DYSENTERY, my father was prostrate on his cot, with another five sick inmates nearby. I sat next to him, watching him; I no longer dared to believe that he could still elude Death. I did all I could to give him hope.

All of a sudden, he sat up and placed his feverish lips against my ear:

"Eliezer . . . I must tell you where I buried the gold and silver . . . In the cellar . . . You know . . ."

And he began talking, faster and faster, afraid of running out of time before he could tell me everything. I tried to tell him that it was not over yet, that we would be going home together, but he no longer wanted to listen to me. He *could* no longer listen to me. He was worn out. Saliva mixed with blood was trickling from his lips. He had closed his eyes. He was gasping more than breathing.

FOR A RATION OF BREAD I was able to exchange cots to be next to my father. When the doctor arrived in the afternoon, I went to tell him that my father was very ill.

"Bring him here!"

I explained that he could not stand up, but the doctor would not listen. And so, with great difficulty I brought my father to him. He stared at him, then asked curtly:

"What do you want?"

"My father is sick," I answered in his place. "Dysentery . . ."

"That's not my business. I'm a surgeon. Go on. Make room for the others!"

My protests were in vain.

"I can't go on, my son . . . Take me back to my bunk."

I took him back and helped him lie down. He was shivering.

"Try to get some sleep, Father. Try to fall asleep . . ."

His breathing was labored. His eyes were closed. But I was convinced that he was seeing everything. That he was seeing the truth in all things.

Another doctor came to the block. My father refused to get up. He knew that it would be of no use.

In fact, that doctor had come only to finish off the patients. I listened to him shouting at them that they were lazy good-for-nothings who only wanted to stay in bed . . . I considered jumping him, strangling him. But I had neither the courage nor the strength. I was riveted to my father's agony. My hands were aching, I was clenching them so hard. To strangle the doctor and the others! To set the whole world on fire! My father's murderers! But even the cry stuck in my throat.

ON MY RETURN from the bread distribution, I found my father crying like a child:

"My son, they are beating me!"

"Who?"

I thought he was delirious.

"Him, the Frenchman . . . and the Pole . . . They beat me : . ."

One more stab to the heart, one more reason to hate. One less reason to live.

"Eliezer . . . Eliezer . . . tell them not to beat me . . . I haven't done anything . . . Why are they beating me?"

I began to insult his neighbors. They mocked me. I promised them bread, soup. They laughed. Then they got angry; they could not stand my father any longer, they said, because he no longer was able to drag himself outside to relieve himself.

THE FOLLOWING DAY, he complained that they had taken his ration of bread.

"While you were asleep?"

"No. I wasn't asleep. They threw themselves on me. They snatched it from me, my bread . . . And they beat me . . . Again . . . I can't go on, my son . . . Give me some water . . ."

I knew that he must not drink. But he pleaded with me so long that I gave in. Water was the worst poison for him, but what else could I do for him? With or without water, it would be over soon anyway . . .

"You, at least, have pity on me . . ."

Have pity on him! I, his only son . . .

A WEEK WENT BY like that.

"Is this your father?" asked the *Blockälteste*.

"Yes."

"He is very sick."

"The doctor won't do anything for him."

He looked me straight in the eye:

"The doctor *cannot* do anything more for him. And neither can you."

He placed his big, hairy hand on my shoulder and added:

"Listen to me, kid. Don't forget that you are in a concentration camp. In this place, it is every man for himself, and you cannot think of others. Not even your father. In this place, there is no such thing as father, brother, friend. Each of us lives and dies alone. Let me give you good advice: stop giving your ration of bread and soup to your old father. You cannot help him anymore. And you are hurting yourself. In fact, you should be getting *his* rations . . ."

I listened to him without interrupting. He was right, I thought deep down, not daring to admit it to myself. Too late to save your old father . . . You could have two rations of bread, two rations of soup . . .

It was only a fraction of a second, but it left me feeling guilty. I ran to get some soup and brought it to my father. But he did not want it. All he wanted was water.

"Don't drink water, eat the soup . . ."

"I'm burning up . . . Why are you so mean to me, my son? . . . Water . . ."

I brought him water. Then I left the block for roll call. But I quickly turned back. I lay down on the upper bunk. The sick were allowed to stay in the block. So I would be sick. I didn't want to leave my father.

All around me, there was silence now, broken only by moaning. In front of the block, the SS were giving orders. An officer passed between the bunks. My father was pleading:

"My son, water . . . I'm burning up . . . My insides . . ."

"Silence, over there!" barked the officer.

"Eliezer," continued my father, "water . . ."

The officer came closer to him and shouted to him to be silent. But my father did not hear. He continued to call me. The officer wielded his club and dealt him a violent blow to the head.

I didn't move. I was afraid, my body was afraid of another blow, this time to *my* head.

My father groaned once more, I heard:

"Eliezer . . ."

I could see that he was still breathing—in gasps. I didn't move.

When I came down from my bunk after roll call, I could see his lips trembling; he was murmuring something. I remained more than an hour leaning over him, looking at him, etching his bloody, broken face into my mind.

Then I had to go to sleep. I climbed into my bunk, above my father, who was still alive. The date was January 28, 1945.

I WOKE UP AT DAWN on January 29. On my father's cot there lay another sick person. They must have taken him away before daybreak and taken him to the crematorium. Perhaps he was still breathing . . .

No prayers were said over his tomb. No candle lit in his memory. His last word had been my name. He had called out to me and I had not answered.

I did not weep, and it pained me that I could not weep. But I was out of tears. And deep inside me, if I could have searched the recesses of my feeble conscience, I might have found something like: Free at last! . . .

I REMAINED IN BUCHENWALD until April 11. I shall not describe my life during that period. It no longer mattered. Since my father's death, nothing mattered to me anymore.

I was transferred to the children's block, where there were six hundred of us.

The front was coming closer.

I spent my days in total idleness. With only one desire: to eat. I no longer thought of my father, or my mother.

From time to time, I would dream. But only about soup, an extra ration of soup.

ON APRIL 5, the wheel of history turned.

It was late afternoon. We were standing inside the block, waiting for an SS to come and count us. He was late. Such lateness was unprecedented in the history of Buchenwald. Something must have happened.

Two hours later, the loudspeakers transmitted an order from the camp Kommandant: all Jews were to gather in the *Appelplatz*.

This was the end! Hitler was about to keep his promise.

The children of our block did as ordered. There was no choice: Gustav, the *Blockälteste*, made it clear with his club . . . But on our way we met some prisoners who whispered to us:

"Go back to your block. The Germans plan to shoot you. Go back and don't move."

We returned to the block. On our way there, we learned that the underground resistance of the camp had made the decision not to abandon the Jews and to prevent their liquidation.

As it was getting late and the confusion was great—countless Jews had been passing as non-Jews—the *Lagerälteste* had decided that a general roll call would take place the next day. Everybody would have to be present.

The roll call took place. The *Lagerkommandant* announced that the Buchenwald camp would be liquidated. Ten blocks of inmates would be evacuated every day. From that moment on, there was no further distribution of bread and soup. And the evacuation began. Every day, a few thousand inmates passed the camp's gate and did not return.

ON APRIL 10, there were still some twenty thousand prisoners in the camp, among them a few hundred children. It was decided to evacuate all of us at once. By evening. Afterward, they would blow up the camp.

And so we were herded onto the huge *Appelplatz*, in ranks of five, waiting for the gate to open. Suddenly, the sirens began to wail. Alert. We went back to the blocks. It was too late to evacuate us that evening. The evacuation was postponed to the next day.

Hunger was tormenting us; we had not eaten for nearly six days except for a few stalks of grass and some potato peels found on the grounds of the kitchens.

At ten o'clock in the morning, the SS took positions throughout the camp and began to herd the last of us toward the *Appelplatz*.

The resistance movement decided at that point to act. Armed men appeared from everywhere. Bursts of gunshots. Grenades exploding. We, the children, remained flat on the floor of the block.

The battle did not last long. Around noon, everything was calm again. The SS had fled and the resistance had taken charge of the camp.

At six o'clock that afternoon, the first American tank stood at the gates of Buchenwald.

OUR FIRST ACT as free men was to throw ourselves onto the provisions. That's all we thought about. No thought of revenge, or of parents. Only of bread.

And even when we were no longer hungry, not one of us thought of revenge. The next day, a few of the young men ran into Weimar to bring back some potatoes and clothes—and to sleep with girls. But still no trace of revenge.

Three days after the liberation of Buchenwald, I became very ill: some form of poisoning. I was transferred to a hospital and spent two weeks between life and death.

One day when I was able to get up, I decided to look at myself in the mirror on the opposite wall. I had not seen myself since the ghetto.

From the depths of the mirror, a corpse was contemplating me.

The look in his eyes as he gazed at me has never left me.

AFTERWORD
MY FATHER'S MESSAGE

ELISHA WIESEL

ADAPTED FROM REMARKS DELIVERED
ON NOVEMBER 30, 2016, AT THE
U.S. HOLOCAUST MEMORIAL MUSEUM,
WASHINGTON, D.C.

W IIEN THE MOMENT COMES," my father told me a year ago, "you will find specific instructions. You will find all the things that need to be taken care of, all the things I want you to know." He didn't tell me what those last wishes were, and I didn't ask. I wasn't ready to contemplate it. I wanted him to focus on living, not on dying. But he gave me the combination to his safe, and I wrote it down.

After my father died, I looked everywhere for these instructions. There was no message, not one that I could find. Not in his safe, not in the files on his computer, not in the papers in his desk drawers.

So I look for his message in the weekly Torah readings. My father asked me to say Kaddish for him, so I spend a lot of time in shul these days.

And I find him there. I see him in the great figures of Jewish history who fired his imagination: Jacob, the man who wrestled with God . . . Isaac, the child who walked off the sacrificial altar . . . And Abraham most of all, a man of profound humility who tirelessly set the standard for devotion to God and, through it, kindness to his fellow man.

I see myself together with my father in the Akedah, the Binding of Isaac, a story, perhaps *the* story, of a father and son. As Isaac's life hangs in the balance while his father and God test each other, so too does mine.

Abraham is a man who has seen entire cities destroyed by a judging God. And as he binds his own son, he contemplates the end of his line. My father sees his whole world consumed by flames. He cannot contemplate bringing another Jewish child into being. Can you feel my fate hang in the balance as Man and God judge each other and all of Creation? Up on the mountain, the knife is raised. And down in the darkness of the valley that is a survivor's life, my father decides that I will not exist.

The Akedah has defied explanation more than any other passage in the Torah. It is a conundrum, a philosophical singularity. Not even the most learned commentator can satisfactorily explain why God subjects Abraham to this terrible test. I dare them to try to explain the tests my father has been through, or on what basis he found hope for the future. But listen:

וַיֹּאמֶר יִצְחָק אֶל-אַבְרָהָם אָבִיו, וַיֹּאמֶר אָבִי, וַיֹּאמֶר, הִנֶּנִּי בְנִי.

"Father?" the son asks. "*Hineni, bni*—I am here, my son," the father answers.

Does my father hear my unconceived voice calling to him backward through time, does it momentarily flash into his consciousness? Is it the arguments of his revered teacher, Professor Shaul Lieberman, or the Lubavitcher Rebbe, telling him he cannot lead a full Jewish life without a family? Or is the angel who stays my father's hand here with us tonight, is it my mother who finally returns him to the earthbound preoccupations of the living, to be his partner in life, to care for a next generation and for those in need of his example?

Hineni, my father answers—and in saying it, he decides to live. He marries. He has a child. He continues the compact between generations.

HINENI, my father cried loud and clear to us all. I am here. I survived. And I will not be silent.

He told the world what he saw and what he feared would come if it did not listen. And I stand before you today as the improbable evidence, a witness that, by my very existence, affirms my father's unrelenting optimism and hope for our species.

His optimism. His hope. Because for someone who had seen the worst, my father tended to see the best in people.

He saw the best in me, even when I didn't. He saw the burden that being his son placed on me when I was younger, and he did what he could to lighten it.

He saw the best in the Jewish sages, even when I didn't. When I challenged him once on some of the Torah's harshest passages, he would say, "Some parts were for a different time and place; why not focus instead on the parts that are timeless?"

And he saw the best in this country. He saw it through the eyes of a survivor rescued by U.S. servicemen, through the eyes of an immigrant who had nothing, who was given a state when he was stateless.

He believed strongly in the role of this museum in broadcasting the dangers of viewing the "other" with distrust and suspicion.

And, in his relentless battle for compassion and fair treatment of the "other," he acted in keeping with thousands of years of Jewish tradition commemorating the Exodus from Egypt. For here is what we are commanded to do, over and over again:

וְגֵר לֹא-תוֹנֶה, וְלֹא תִלְחָצֶנּוּ: כִּי-גֵרִים הֱיִיתֶם, בְּאֶרֶץ מִצְרָיִם.

"And a stranger shalt thou not wrong, neither shalt thou oppress him; for ye were strangers in the land of Egypt."

וְגֵר, לֹא תִלְחָץ; וְאַתֶּם, יְדַעְתֶּם אֶת נֶפֶשׁ הַגֵּר—כִּי-גֵרִים הֱיִיתֶם, בְּאֶרֶץ מִצְרָיִם.

"And a stranger shalt thou not oppress; for ye know the heart of a stranger, seeing ye were strangers in the land of Egypt."

כְּאֶזְרָח מִכֶּם יִהְיֶה לָכֶם הַגֵּר הַגָּר אִתְּכֶם, וְאָהַבְתָּ לוֹ כָּמוֹךָ—כִּי-גֵרִים הֱיִיתֶם, בְּאֶרֶץ מִצְרָיִם.

"The stranger that sojourneth with you shall be unto you as the home-born among you, and thou shalt love him as thyself; for ye were strangers in the land of Egypt."

The message is clear.

When Syrian refugees need our help, we must help them.

When Muslims in our midst are made to feel they won't have the same rights as the rest of us, we must embrace them.

When children of hardworking and law-abiding undocumented immigrants fear deportation, we must insist on adding compassion into the equation.

When women are made to feel that they are objects rather than people, when our daughters are diminished in any way, we must protest.

When African American citizens feel they are strangers in the eyes of the law, and policemen feel estranged from the communities they serve, we must seek to rebuild that trust in both directions.

When the LGBTQ community feel they are at risk of being terrorized, we must let them know we stand with them.

And when the State of Israel is singled out by the United Nations and BDS activists and treated as the world's villain simply for making sure that Jews will never again be without a homeland—we must let Israel know she is not a stranger in foreign affairs but an essential partner in the global struggle for democracy.

In this museum—whose fundamental premise is that we must never again allow ourselves to condemn the "other" simply for being the "other"—is there any question about the scope of the work ahead for all of us?

And as we do all this, we must acknowledge that there is a danger. As we seek to change hearts and minds and create a more tolerant society, there is a danger that we may treat those whose opinions we find offensive as the "other" in turn. This was not my father's way. He was not a shouter; he did not belittle those he disagreed with. He spoke to them. He listened. He asked questions—sometimes pointed questions, but more often open-ended ones. He led by example.

But let us return to Abraham and Isaac. Thousands of years ago, two men are coming down the mountain. One sage remarks on the language, the fact that the same words are used for both the coming and the going. Abraham and Isaac walked up together, they walked down together. Their relationship was not defeated by the momentous experience they had just undergone. My father and I too loved each other across a gulf of understanding that should have been hard to bridge—he, who had everything taken away from him as a child; I, to whom everything was given.

I never found the message he left behind.

But maybe that expression of his hopes and dreams was there in his study after all—in the Torah scroll he kept in his office, in his thousands of books, in the body of learning of which his spirit has now eternally become a part. I believe that's a part of it.

But what I also believe is that each one of you who knew him, who read his first book, *Night*, or his many other books, or heard his speeches, or studied with him, each of you who believe in what he stood for and have your own story—each of you retains a shard of that message. And when we come together as we do tonight, that message is so much clearer.

May his memory be a blessing to us all.

WILL THE WORLD EVER LEARN?

COMMEMORATION OF THE SIXTIETH ANNIVERSARY OF THE LIBERATION OF THE NAZI DEATH CAMPS

ELIE WIESEL

SPECIAL SESSION
OF THE UNITED NATIONS
GENERAL ASSEMBLY,
JANUARY 24, 2005

M R. PRESIDENT of the General Assembly, my friend Mr. Secretary General, foreign ministers, ambassadors, excellencies, fellow survivors, friends:

The man who stands before you this morning feels deeply privileged. A teacher and writer, he speaks and writes as a witness to a crime committed in the heart of European Christendom and civilization by a brutal dictatorial regime—a crime of unprecedented cruelty in which all segments of government participated.

When speaking about that era of darkness, the witness encounters difficulties. His words become obstacles rather than vehicles; he writes not *with* words but *against* words. For there are no words to describe what the victims felt when death was the norm and life a miracle. Still, whether you know it or not, his memory is part of yours.

I speak to you as a son of an ancient people, the only people of antiquity to have survived antiquity, the Jewish people, which, throughout much of its history, has endured exile and oppression yet has never given up hope of redemption.

As a young adolescent, he saw what no human being should

have to see: the triumph of political fanaticism and ideological hatred of those who were different. He saw multitudes of human beings humiliated, isolated, tormented, tortured, and murdered. They were overwhelmingly Jews, but there were others. And those who committed these crimes were not vulgar underworld thugs but men with high government, academic, industrial, and medical positions in Germany. In recent years, that nation has become a true democracy. But the question remains open: In those dark years, what motivated so many brilliant and committed public servants to invent such horrors? By its scope and magnitude, by its sheer weight of numbers, by the impact of so much humiliation and pain, in spite of being the most documented tragedy in the annals of history, Auschwitz still defies language and understanding.

Let me evoke those times:

Babies used as target practice by SS men . . . Adolescents condemned never to grow old . . . Parents watching their children thrown into burning pits . . . Immense solitude engulfing an entire people . . . Infinite despair haunting our days and our dreams sixty years later . . .

When did what we so poorly call the Holocaust begin? In 1938, during Kristallnacht? In 1939, perhaps, when a German ship, the *St. Louis*, with nearly a thousand German Jewish refugees aboard, was turned back from America's shores? Or was it when the first massacres occurred in Babi Yar?

We still ask: What was Auschwitz, an end or a beginning? An apocalyptic consequence of centuries-old bigotry and hatred, or the final convulsion of demonic forces in human nature?

A creation parallel to God's—a world with its own antinomian United Nations of people of different nationalities, traditions, cultures, socioeconomic spheres, philosophical disciplines, speaking many languages, clinging to a variety of faiths and memories. They were grown-ups or young, but inside that world there were no children and no grandparents; they had already perished.

As I have said many times: Not all victims were Jews, but all Jews were victims. For the first time in recorded history, to *be* became a crime. Their birth became their death sentence. Correction: Jewish children were condemned to die even *before* they were born. What the enemy sought was to put an end to Jewish history; what he wanted was a new world implacably, irrevocably devoid of Jews. Hence Auschwitz, Ponar, Treblinka, Belzec, Chelmno, and Sobibor: dark factories of death erected for the Final Solution. Killers came there to kill and victims to die.

That was Auschwitz, an executioner's ideal of a kingdom of absolute evil and malediction, with its princes and beggars, philosophers and theologians, politicians and artists, a place where to lose a piece of bread meant moving a step closer to death, and a smile from a friend, another day of promise.

At the time, the witness tried to understand. He still does not: How was such calculated evil, such bottomless and pointless cruelty, possible? Had creation gone mad? Had God covered His face? A religious person cannot conceive of Auschwitz either with or without God. But what about man? How could intelligent, educated, or simple law-abiding citizens fire machine guns at hundreds of children and their parents, and in the evening enjoy a cadence by Schiller, a partita by Bach?

Turning point or watershed, that catastrophe, which has traumatized history, has forever changed man's perception of responsibility toward other human beings. The sad, terrible fact is that it could have been prevented. Had the Western nations intervened when Hitler occupied Czechoslovakia and Austria; had America accepted more Jewish refugees from Europe; had Britain allowed more Jews to return to their ancestral land; had the Allies bombed the railways leading to Birkenau at the time when ten thousand Hungarian Jews—men, women, and infants—were assassinated day after day, our tragedy might have been avoided, its scope surely diminished.

This shameful indifference we must remember, just as we must remember to thank the few heroic individuals who, like Raoul Wallenberg, risked their lives to save Jews. We shall also always remember the armies that liberated Europe and the soldiers who liberated the death camps, the Americans in Buchenwald, the Russians in Auschwitz, and the British in Belsen. But for many victims they all came too late. That we must also remember.

When the American Third Army liberated Buchenwald, there was no joy in our heart: only pain. We did not sing, we did not celebrate. We had just enough strength to recite the Kaddish.

And now, sixty years later, you, who represent the entire world community, listen to the words of the witness. Like Jeremiah and Job, we could have cried, "And cursed be the days dominated by injustice and violence." We could have chosen vengeance. We did not. Hatred is degrading and vengeance demeaning. They are diseases. Their history is dominated by death.

The Jewish witness speaks of his people's suffering as a warning. He sounds the alarm so as to prevent these things being done to others. Had the world listened to our testimonies, the tragedies of Cambodia, Bosnia, Rwanda, and Darfur might have been avoided.

Oh yes, the witness knows that for the dead it is too late; for them, abandoned by God and betrayed by humanity, victory came much too late. But it is not too late for today's children, ours and yours. It is for their sake alone that we bear witness. It is for their sake that we are duty-bound to denounce anti-Semitism, bigotry, racism, and religious or ethnic hatred. Those who today preach and practice the cult of death, using suicide terrorism, the scourge of this new century, must be condemned for crimes against humanity. Suffering confers no privileges; it is what one does with suffering that matters. Yes, the past is in the present, but the future is still in our hands.

Remember: those who survived Auschwitz advocate hope, not despair; generosity, not rancor or bitterness; gratitude, not violence. We must be engaged; we must reject indifference as an option. Indifference always helps the aggressor, never his victims. And what is memory if not a noble and necessary response to and against indifference?

But . . . will the world ever learn?

THE NOBEL PEACE PRIZE
ACCEPTANCE SPEECH

ELIE WIESEL

DELIVERED IN OSLO, NORWAY,
DECEMBER 10, 1986

Y OUR MAJESTY, Your Royal Highnesses, Your Excellencies, Chairman Aarvik, members of the Nobel Committee, ladies and gentlemen:

Words of gratitude. First to our common Creator. This is what the Jewish tradition commands us to do. At special occasions, one is duty-bound to recite the following prayer: "*Barukh atah Adonai . . . shehekhyanu vekiymanu vehigianu lazman hazeh*"—"Blessed be Thou . . . for giving us life, for sustaining us, and for enabling us to reach this day."

Then—thank you, Chairman Aarvik, for the depth of your eloquence. And for the generosity of your gesture. Thank you for building bridges between people and generations. Thank you, above all, for helping humankind make peace its most urgent and noble aspiration.

I am moved, deeply moved by your words, Chairman Aarvik. And it is with a profound sense of humility that I accept the honor—the highest there is—that you have chosen to bestow upon me. I know your choice transcends my person.

Do I have the right to represent the multitudes who have perished? Do I have the right to accept this great honor on their behalf? I do not. No one may speak for the dead, no one may interpret their mutilated dreams and visions. And yet, I sense their presence. I always do—and at this moment more than ever. The presence of my parents, that of my little sister. The presence of my teachers, my friends, my companions . . .

This honor belongs to all the survivors and their children and, through us, to the Jewish people with whose destiny I have always identified.

I remember: it happened yesterday, or eternities ago. A young Jewish boy discovered the Kingdom of Night. I remember his bewilderment, I remember his anguish. It all happened so fast. The ghetto. The deportation. The sealed cattle car. The fiery altar upon which the history of our people and the future of mankind were meant to be sacrificed.

I remember he asked his father: "Can this be true? This is the twentieth century, not the Middle Ages. Who would allow such crimes to be committed? How could the world remain silent?"

And now the boy is turning to me. "Tell me," he asks, "what have you done with my future, what have you done with your life?" And I tell him that I have tried. That I have tried to keep memory alive, that I have tried to fight those who would forget. Because if we forget, we are guilty, we are accomplices.

And then I explain to him how naïve we were, that the world did know and remained silent. And that is why I swore never to be silent whenever and wherever human beings endure suffering and humiliation. We must take sides. Neutrality helps the oppressor, never the victim. Silence encourages the tormentor, never the tormented. Sometimes we must interfere. When human lives are endangered, when human dignity is in jeopardy, national borders and sensitivities become irrelevant. Wherever men and women are persecuted because of their race, religion, or political views, that place must—at that moment—become the center of the universe.

Of course, since I am a Jew profoundly rooted in my people's memory and tradition, my first response is to Jewish fears, Jewish needs, Jewish crises. For I belong to a traumatized generation, one that experienced the abandonment and solitude of our people. It would be unnatural for me not to make Jewish priorities my own: Israel, Soviet Jewry, Jews in Arab lands . . . But others are important to me. Apartheid is, in my view, as abhorrent as anti-Semitism. To me, Andrei Sakharov's isolation is as much a disgrace as Josef Biegun's imprisonment and Ida Nudel's exile. As is the denial of Solidarity and its leader Lech Walesa's right to dissent. And Nelson Mandela's interminable imprisonment.

There is so much injustice and suffering crying out for our attention: victims of hunger, of racism and political persecution—in Chile, for instance, or in Ethiopia—writers and poets, prisoners in so many lands governed by the left and by the right.

Human rights are being violated on every continent. More people are oppressed than free. How can one not be sensitive to their plight? Human suffering anywhere concerns men and women everywhere. That applies also to Palestinians, to whose plight I am sensitive but whose methods I deplore when they lead to violence. Violence is not the answer. Terrorism is the most dangerous of answers. They are frustrated, that is understandable, something must be done. The refugees and their misery. The children and their fear. The uprooted and their hopelessness. Something must be done about their situation. Both the Jewish people and the Palestinian people have lost too many sons and daughters and have shed too much blood. This must stop, and all attempts to stop it must be encouraged. Israel will cooperate, I am sure of that. I trust Israel, for I have faith in the Jewish people. Let Israel be given a chance, let hatred and danger be removed from their horizons, and there will be peace in and around the Holy Land. Please understand my deep and total commitment to Israel: if you could remember what I remember, you would understand. Israel is the only nation in the world whose existence is threatened. Should Israel lose but one war, it would mean her end and ours as well. But I have faith. Faith in the God of Abraham, Isaac, and Jacob, and even in His creation. Without it no action would be possible. And action is the only remedy to indifference, the most insidious danger of all. Isn't that the meaning of Alfred Nobel's legacy? Wasn't his fear of war a shield against war?

There is so much to be done, there is so much that can be done. One person—a Raoul Wallenberg, an Albert Schweitzer, a Martin Luther King Jr.—one person of integrity can make a difference, a difference of life and death. As long as one dissident is in prison, our freedom will not be true. As long as one child is hungry, our life will be filled with anguish and shame. What these victims need above all is to know that they are not alone; that we are not forgetting them, that when their voices are stifled we shall lend them ours, that, while their freedom depends on ours, the quality of our freedom depends on theirs.

This is what I say to the young Jewish boy wondering what I have done with his years. It is in his name that I speak to you and that I express to you my deepest gratitude as one who has emerged from the Kingdom of Night. We know that every moment is a moment of grace, every hour an offering; not to share them would mean to betray them.

Our lives no longer belong to us alone; they belong to all those who need us desperately.

Thank you, Chairman Aarvik. Thank you, members of the Nobel Committee. Thank you, people of Norway, for declaring on this singular occasion that our survival has meaning for mankind.

THE NOBEL LECTURE
HOPE, DESPAIR, AND MEMORY

ELIE WIESEL

DELIVERED IN OSLO, NORWAY,
DECEMBER 11, 1986

*A*NI MAAMIN, I believe . . . I believe in the coming of the Messiah . . . I believe in the hope for a future, just as I believe in the irresistible power of memory.

A Hasidic legend tells us that the great Rabbi Israel Baal Shem Tov, Master of the Good Name, also known as the Besht, undertook an urgent and perilous mission. He wanted to hasten the coming of the Messiah. The Jewish people, all humanity, were suffering too much, beset by too many evils. They had to be saved, and swiftly. For having tried to meddle with history, the Besht was punished. He was banished along with his faithful servant to a distant island.

In despair, the servant implored his master to exercise his mysterious powers in order to bring them both home. "Impossible," the Besht replied. "My powers, my mystical powers, have been taken from me."

"Then, please, say a prayer, recite a litany, work a miracle."

"Impossible," the Master replied. "I have forgotten everything." And so they both fell to weeping.

Suddenly the Master turned to his servant and asked, "My friend, remind me of a prayer, any prayer."

"If only I could," said the servant. "I too have forgotten everything."

"Everything, absolutely everything?"

"Everything," said the servant, "except . . ."

"Except what?"

"Except the alphabet!"

At that the Besht cried out joyfully, "Then what are you waiting for? Begin reciting the alphabet, and I shall repeat after you." And together the two exiled men began to recite, at first in whispers, then more loudly, the Hebrew equivalent of the ABCs: "*Aleph beth gimmel,*" and over again, "*Aleph beth gimmel,*" each time more vigorously, more fervently, until the Besht ultimately regained his memory and thus his powers.

I love this story, for I love stories. But I especially love this one because it illustrates the messianic exhortation and expectation which remains my own. It also illustrates the importance of friendship to man's ability to transcend his condition. I love it most of all because it emphasizes the mystical power of memory. Without memory, our existence would be barren and opaque, like a prison cell into which no light penetrates, like a tomb that rejects the living. Memory served and saved Besht, and if anything can, it is memory that will save humanity. For me, hope without memory is like memory without hope.

Just as man cannot live without dreams, man cannot live without expectations. If dreams reflect the past, hope summons the future. Does this mean that our future can be built on a rejection of the past? Surely such a choice is not necessary. The two are not incompatible. The opposite of the past is not the future but the absence of future; the opposite of the future is not the past but the absence of the past. The loss of one is equivalent to the sacrifice of the other.

A recollection. The time: after the war. The place: Paris. A young man, a young Jew, struggles to readjust to life. His mother, his father, his small sister are gone. He is alone. On the verge of despair. And yet he does not give up. On the contrary, this young Jew strives to find a place among the living. He acquires a new language. He makes a few friends who, like himself, believe that the memory of evil will serve as a shield against evil, that the memory of death will serve as a shield against death. This he must believe. It is a kind of existential belief—like Kierkegaard, he *must* believe in it in order to go on. For he has just returned from a universe where God, betrayed by His creatures, covered His face in order not to see. Mankind, jewel of His creation, had succeeded in building an inverted Tower of Babel, reaching not toward heaven but toward an anti-heaven, there to create a parallel society, a new "creation" with its own princes and gods, laws and principles, jailers and prisoners. A world where the past no longer counted—no longer meant anything.

Stripped of possessions, all human ties severed, the prisoners found themselves in a social and cultural void. "Forget," they were told. "Forget where you came from; forget who you were. Only the present matters." But the present was only a blink of God's eye. The slaughterer himself was God-like, almighty: it was he who decided who would live and who would die, who would be tortured and who would be rewarded. Night after night, seemingly endless processions vanished into the flames, lighting up the sky. Fear dominated the universe. Indeed, this was another universe; the very laws of nature had been transformed. Children looked like old men, old men whimpered like children. Men and women from every corner of Europe were suddenly reduced to nameless and faceless creatures, desperate for the same ration of bread or soup, dreading the same end. Even their silence was the same, for it resounded with the memory of those who were gone. Life in this accursed universe was so distorted, so unnatural, that a new species evolved. Waking among the dead, one wondered if one were still alive.

And yet some of us remember that real despair did not seize us until later, until after the war. Psychiatrists refer to this as "latency." We need a certain period between the event and the response to the event, because the immediate response would be overwhelming, tragic; and, inevitably, the person going through the experience would be crushed by it. We needed time to rethink and reevaluate our acquired certainties.

As we emerged from the nightmare, we began to search for meaning: All those doctors of law or medicine or theology, all those lovers of art and poetry, of Bach and Goethe, who coldly and deliberately ordered the massacres and participated in them, what did their metamorphosis signify? Could anything explain their loss of ethical, cultural, and religious memory? How could we ever understand the passivity of the onlookers and, yes, the silence of the Allies?

To this day, I don't understand how the enemy drove ten thousand Jews to Babi Yar day after day between Rosh Hashanah (the New Year) and Yom Kippur (the Day of Atonement). Babi Yar is not *outside* Kiev, Babi Yar is *in* Kiev—and they were all machine-gunned. They went through the streets, people saw them marching, heard the machine guns. What happened to the people? Did they become dead, blind, mute? I cannot understand their indifference. Nor can I understand, and I say so with pain in my heart, the silence of people who were good people. Roosevelt was a good man and Churchill was a great man. They had the courage then to fight the mighty Hitler and his powerful armies. But when it came to saving Jews, somehow the principles of humanity no longer applied. What happened? What made Roosevelt a different person? I do not understand it. And to me, a Jew who comes from a deeply religious background, there was the question of questions: *Where was God in all this?* It seemed as impossible to conceive of Auschwitz with God as to conceive of Auschwitz without God. The tragedy of the believer is much greater than the tragedy of the nonbeliever. But after the war, whether one was a believer or not, everything had to be reassessed, because everything had changed. With one stroke, mankind's achievements seemed to have been erased.

Was Auschwitz a consequence of "civilization" or was it an aberration? All we know is that Auschwitz called that civilization into question, as it called into question everything that had preceded Auschwitz. Scientific abstraction, social and economic contention, nationalism, xenophobia, religious fanaticism, racism, mass hysteria, and, of course, anti-Semitism, both religious and social—all found their ultimate expression in Auschwitz.

The next question my generation had to face was: Why go on? If memory continually brought us back to the altar, why build a home? Why go to school? Why reach out to others? Why make friends? Why trust? Why have faith in anyone or in yourself? How can I be sure that tomorrow the sun will shine when night seems eternal? And why bring children into a world in which God and man betrayed their trust in one another?

And yet, it is surely human to forget, even to want to forget. The ancients saw it as a divine gift. Indeed, if memory helps us to survive, forgetting allows us to go on living. How could we go on with our daily lives if we remained constantly aware of the dangers and ghosts surrounding us? The Talmud even tells us that without the ability to forget, man would soon cease to learn. Without the ability to forget, man would live in a permanent, paralyzing fear of death. Only God and God alone can and must remember everything all the time.

How are we to reconcile our supreme duty toward memory with the need to forget that is essential to life? No generation has had to confront this paradox with such urgency. The survivors wanted to communicate everything to the living: the victims' solitude and sorrow, the tears of mothers driven to madness, the prayers of the doomed beneath a fiery sky. They needed to tell of the beggar who, in a sealed cattle car, began to sing as an offering to his companions, and of the little girl who, hugging her grandmother, whispered: "Grandmother, don't be afraid, don't be sorry to die—I'm not. It's not worth going on living."

Each one of us felt compelled to recall every story, every encounter. Each one of us felt compelled to bear witness. Such were the wishes of the dying, the testament of the dead. Since the so-called civilized world had no use for their lives, then let it be inhabited by their deaths.

The great Jewish historian Shimon Dubnov served as our guide and inspiration. Until the moment of his death, he said over and over again in Yiddish to his companions in the Riga ghetto: *"Yidden, shreibt un fershreibt!"* ("Jews, write it all down!") His words were heeded. Overnight, countless victims became chroniclers and historians in the ghettos, even in the death camps. Even members of the Sonderkommandos, those inmates forced to burn their fellow inmates' corpses before being burned in turn, left behind extraordinary documents. To testify became an obsession. They left us poems and letters, diaries, fragments of testimony, some known throughout the world, others that should be published but remain unpublished.

After the war, we reassured ourselves that it would be enough to relate a single night in Auschwitz, to tell of the cruelty, the senselessness of murder, and the outrage born of apathy; it would be enough to find the right word and the propitious moment to say it, to shake humanity out of its indifference, and to keep the torturer from torturing ever again. We thought it would be enough to read the world a poem written by a child in the Theresienstadt ghetto to ensure that no child anywhere would ever again have to endure hunger or fear or solitude. It would be enough to describe a death camp "selection" to prevent the human right to dignity from being violated ever again.

We thought it would be enough to tell of the tidal wave of hatred that broke over the Jewish people, to have men everywhere decide once and for all to put an end to hatred of anyone who is "different"—whether black or white, Jew or Arab, Christian or Muslim—anyone whose orientation differs politically, philosophically, sexually. A naïve undertaking? Of course. But not without a certain logic.

We tried. It was not easy. At first, because of the language: language failed us. We would have to invent a new vocabulary, for our own words were inadequate, anemic.

And then, too, the people around us refused to listen; and even those who listened refused to believe; and even those who believed could not comprehend. Of course they could not. Nobody could. The experience of the camps defies comprehension. Can you understand, can anyone understand, how a nation of such culture, of such power, could all of a sudden invent death camps, death factories, and mobilize its entire industry, its science, its philosophy, its passion, to kill Jewish people? For what? I cannot understand; even from *their* viewpoint it was madness. In 1944, when they were losing the war, they gave priority to trains leading Jews to their deaths over military trains bringing soldiers and weapons to the front. That doesn't make sense. But it was going on to the very last day. Wouldn't the story of their irrational criminal behavior prevent irrational crimes against humanity elsewhere?

So we tried. Perhaps if we were to tell the tale things would change. Have we failed? I often think we have. If someone had told us in 1945 that in our lifetime religious wars would rage on virtually every continent, that thousands of children would once again be dying of starvation, we would not have believed it. Or that racism and fanaticism would flourish once again. Nor would we have believed there would be governments that would deprive men and women of their basic rights merely because they dared to dissent. Governments of the right and of the left still subject those who dissent—writers, scientists, intellectuals—to torture and persecution. How is one to explain all this unless we consider the defeat of memory?

How is one to explain any of it? The outrage of apartheid, which continues unabated? Racism in itself is dreadful, but when it pretends to be legal, and therefore just, it becomes even more repugnant. Without comparing apartheid to Nazism and to its "Final Solution"—for that defies all comparison—one cannot help but assign the two systems, in their supposed legality, to the same camp. What about the outrage of terrorism? Of the hostages in Iran, the cold-blooded massacre in the synagogues in Istanbul, Paris, and Vienna, the senseless deaths in the streets of Beirut?

Terrorism must be outlawed by all civilized nations—not explained or rationalized but fought and eradicated. Nothing can, nothing will, justify the murder of innocent people and helpless children . . . and the outrage of preventing men and women, marvelous men and women like Andrei Sakharov, Vladimir and Masha Slepak, Ida Nudel, Josef Biegun, Victor Brailovsky, Zakhar Zonshein, Juli Edelstein, and all the others known and unknown, from leaving their country.

Yesterday afternoon, when I left this hall with its overwhelming emotional aspect, my wife and I went to our hotel and began calling refuseniks in the Soviet Union. That is what we did all afternoon. We wanted them to know that, especially on this day, we were thinking not only of our joy but also of their plight. We went on calling, one after another. At one point they began calling back. The whole afternoon was a dialogue of human solidarity. If ever your prize had concrete, immediate meaning, distinguished Members of the Committee, it was yesterday afternoon: to those Jews in Russia it meant that here in this place we care, we think of them, and we shall never forget.

As a Jew, I must also speak about Israel. After two thousand years of exile and thirty-eight years of sovereignty, Israel still does not enjoy peace. I would like to see the people of Israel, my people, establish the foundation for a constructive relationship with all its Arab neighbors, as it has done with Egypt. We must see to it that the Jewish people in Israel and all people in the Middle East enjoy some measure of peace and hope . . . at last. We must exert pressure on all those in power to come to terms.

And here we come back to memory. We must remember the suffering of my people, as we must remember that of the Ethiopians, the Cambodians, the Boat People, the Palestinians, the Miskito Indians, the Argentinian *"desaparecidos"*—the list seems endless.

Let us remember Job, who, having lost everything—his children, his friends, his possessions, and even his argument with God—still found the strength to begin again, to rebuild his life. Job was determined not to repudiate the creation, however imperfect, that God had entrusted to him.

Job, our ancestor. Job, our contemporary. Everything in our tradition tells us that Job was not a Jew, but this suffering concerns us. It concerns us so much that we have taken his language into our liturgy. His ordeal concerns all humanity. Did he ever lose his faith? If so, he rediscovered it within his rebellion. He demonstrated that faith is essentially an act of rebellion, and that hope is possible beyond despair. The source of his hope was memory, as it must be ours. Because I remember, I despair. Because I remember, I have the duty to reject despair.

I remember the killers and I despair; I remember the victims and, on their behalf and for their sake and for their children's sake, I must invent a thousand and one reasons to hope.

There may be times when we are powerless to prevent injustice, but there must never be a time when we fail to protest. The Talmud tells us that by saving a single human being—and there are two versions: one version says a single Jewish human being and the other version says any human being—man can save the world. We may be powerless to open all the jails and free all the prisoners, but by declaring our solidarity with one prisoner, we indict all jailers. None of us is in a position to eliminate war, but it is our obligation to denounce it and expose it in all its hideousness. War leaves no victors, only victims.

I began with the story of the Besht. And, like the Besht, mankind needs to remember more than ever. Mankind needs peace more than ever, for our entire planet, threatened by nuclear war, is in danger of total elimination; a destruction, an annihilation, only man can provoke, only man can prevent. It is all up to us. The lesson, the only lesson that I have learned from my experiences, is twofold: First, that there are no plausible answers to what we have endured. There are no theological answers, there are no psychological answers, there are no literary answers, there are no philosophical answers, there are no religious answers. The only conceivable answer is a *moral* answer. This means there must be a moral element in whatever we do. Second, that just as despair can be given to me only by another human being, hope too can be given to me only by another human being. Mankind must remember also, and above all, that, like hope and whatever hope signifies, peace is not God's gift to all his creatures. Peace is a very special gift—it is our gift to each other. And so *Ani maamin*—I believe—that we must have hope for one another also because of one another. And *Ani maamin*—I believe—that because of our children and theirs we should be worthy of that hope, of that redemption, and of some measure of peace.

I thank you.

A Note About the Author

Elie Wiesel was born in 1928 in Sighet, Transylvania. At the age of fifteen, he was deported to Auschwitz, where his mother and younger sister perished. Elie and his father were later transported to Buchenwald, where his father died shortly before the camp was liberated in April 1945.

After the war, Elie Wiesel began to rebuild his life in Paris, where he became a journalist and a choirmaster. During an interview with the eminent Catholic author François Mauriac, he was persuaded to write about his experiences in the death camps. The result was his internationally acclaimed memoir *La Nuit*, or *Night*, which has since been translated into thirty languages.

Night was the first of an astonishing sixty books that Elie Wiesel would eventually publish. It was also his most crucial volume. "If in my lifetime I would write only one book," he said, "this would be the one . . . There are those who tell me that I survived in order to write this text."

In his Nobel presentation speech, Egil Aarvik, chairman of the Norwegian Nobel Committee, said in Oslo on December 8, 1986, "Elie Wiesel was rescued from the ashes of Auschwitz after storm and fire had ravaged his life . . . In time he realized that his life could have purpose: that he was to be a witness, the one who would pass on the account of what had happened so that the dead would not have died in vain and so the living could learn." Soon after receiving the Nobel Peace Prize, Elie Wiesel and his wife, Marion, created the Elie Wiesel Foundation for Humanity to counter indifference, intolerance and injustice throughout the world.

A staunch supporter of human rights, Elie Wiesel worked tirelessly on behalf of numerous groups, from Soviet Jews, Nicaragua's Miskito Indians, and Argentina's *desaparecidos* to Cambodian refugees, the Kurds, and victims of famine in Africa, of apartheid in South Africa, and of ethnic cleansing in the former

Yugoslavia. The United States Holocaust Memorial Museum in Washington, D.C., of which Elie Wiesel was founding chairman, continues to teach the world about the consequences of genocide.

Teaching and study were central to Elie Wiesel's life's work. For forty years, he was the Andrew W. Mellon Professor in the Humanities at Boston University, where he was named University Professor. He was a recipient of numerous honorary degrees and other awards, the Presidential Medal of Freedom, the U.S. Congressional Gold Medal, the Medal of Liberty Award, and the rank of Grand Officer in the French Legion of Honor among them.

Oprah Winfrey, who said *Night* should be "required reading for all humanity," chose it as a selection of her book club in 2006. Forty-five years after publication, *Night* rose to the top of the *New York Times* bestseller list.

Elie Wiesel died on July 2, 2016.